Boost Attacks, Increase Defense, and Restore Your Health with 60 Adventurous Recipes Inspired by the Fan-Favorite Video Game

The Unofficial
GENSHIN
IMPACT
Cookbook

Kierra Sondereker
Nevyana Dimitrova

ULYSSES PRESS

Published by:
Ulysses Press
PO Box 3440
Berkeley, CA 94703
www.ulyssespress.com

ISBN: 978-1-64604-548-8
Library of Congress Control Number: 2023938272

Printed in China
10 9 8 7 6 5 4 3 2 1

Recipes and recipe photographs: Nevyana Dimitrova
Acquisitions editor: Casie Vogel
Managing editor: Claire Chun
Editor: Phyllis Elving
Proofreader: Barbara Schultz
Front cover design: Monique Sterling
Interior design: Winnie Liu
Layout: what!design @ whatweb.com
Artwork: food photographs Nevyana Dimitrova; mountain scenic illustration © Justinas/ AdobeStock; back cover food frame © Vector FX/shutterstock.com

To my older brother, Kyle, who always let me watch him play video games growing up. And to my younger brother, Keadron, who always played LEGO® Star Wars with me on Xbox when we were kids.

These early video game experiences with you led me to my current obsession with Genshin Impact.

—K.S.

* * *

To my beloved family and adoring fiancé, the unwavering pillars of my life. With boundless love and belief in me, you have been my constant support on my culinary journey. Through every recipe, I honor our shared traditions and the precious memories we create together. May these pages serve as a reminder of the immense joy we find in food and the unbreakable bonds that unite us. With all my love.

—N.D.

CONTENTS

INTRODUCTION

Welcome Travelers!

If you've made your way to this cookbook, that means you've finally logged out of Genshin Impact long enough to take a trip to the bookstore, peruse the shelves, and come away with a brand-new cookbook. Or maybe you simply switched over from gaming to your open Amazon cart. Or, lucky you, someone clocked your obsession with Genshin and bought this cookbook for you as a gift. Whatever the case may be, thanks for joining in on the adventure!

When I first started playing Genshin Impact, I could not have survived without many of the dishes found in this cookbook. As a low Adventure Rank Traveler roaming across Teyvat, I remember consuming one Chicken-Mushroom Skewer after the other while going up against a single hilichurl, or cooking Fried Radish on a Stick in bulk in the hopes of dealing anything near 1,000 damage.

Now at AR 59, I'm proud to say I rely much less on food to heal, attack, and defend myself and my team. But that doesn't stop me from constantly cooking dishes to get my weekly Battle Pass rewards—all while wishing I could taste these dishes in real life. I mean, how can they make animated food look so good? So I thought to myself, why not bring the food from my favorite game to life? I've already clocked an unmention-able number of hours playing Genshin, so what's a few more? And thus the idea for this cookbook was born.

So I invite you all to set out on yet another adventure—this time a culinary one! I've collected some of my favorite dishes from the hills of Mondstadt, the deserts of Sumeru, the mountains of Liyue, and more, and I worked with the wonderful recipe developer and food photographer Nevyana Dimitrova to turn them into step-by-step, real-life recipes that you can use to put your cooking skills to the test.

And if you're new to Genshin Impact or have never even heard of it before this (no shade, but you should rectify that as soon as possible), don't think for one second that this cookbook isn't for you. The world of Teyvat is based on real-life cultures from around the globe, so the recipes within these pages will teach you how to make some of the best dishes out there—such as delicious Chicken Biryani and Simple Onigiri.

Whether you're a diehard Genshin Impact fan like me or are simply looking for some fun new recipes to test out, I guarantee that you'll find something in this cookbook to love. Now get out your pots and pans, light your fires, and prepare to make the tastiest dishes known to humans, gods, and flying white-haired companions alike!

APPETIZERS AND SIDES

1 tablespoon dried oregano

1 tablespoon Dijon mustard

½ teaspoon dried thyme

juice from 1 lemon

3 cloves garlic, minced

2 tablespoons olive oil

1 tablespoon
smoked paprika

¼ cup soy sauce

1 tablespoon maple syrup

3 tablespoons orange juice

¼ cup chicken stock

½ teaspoon pepper

2 boneless, skinless
chicken breasts

1 pound whole cremini
mushrooms

SPECIAL EQUIPMENT

8 to 10 bamboo or
metal skewers

GRILLED CHICKEN SKEWERS

We're starting off with a dish that's hard to mess up. Maybe that's why it's the favorite food of one particularly unlucky adventurer we all know and love. This simple yet completely satisfying recipe is perfect for Travelers just starting out on the culinary journey!

1. In a large bowl, mix together all the ingredients except the chicken and mushrooms to create a marinade.

2. Cut the chicken breasts into bite-size pieces. Place the chicken and mushrooms in the bowl of marinade and stir until thoroughly coated. Cover and refrigerate for 4 to 10 hours, stirring occasionally.

3. If you're using bamboo skewers, soak them in water for a few minutes right before the chicken and mushrooms are done marinating to keep them from burning when it comes time to cook. Then pat dry.

4. Thread the chicken and mushrooms on the skewers, discarding any remaining marinade. Grill on high heat until cooked, 5 to 7 minutes, or bake in the oven at 430°F for 8 to 10 minutes. Enjoy!

✦ ✦ ✦

SERVES: 4 | **PREP TIME:** 10 minutes + 4 to 10 hours for marinating | **COOK TIME:** 5 to 10 minutes

1 large white daikon radish

pinch of salt + more, for sprinkling

2 large eggs

¾ cup all-purpose flour

1 green onion, thinly sliced

1 teaspoon vegetable stock powder

1 teaspoon minced fresh ginger or ginger paste

1 teaspoon garlic powder

1 teaspoon onion powder

1 teaspoon paprika

pinch of pepper

vegetable oil, for frying

FRIED RADISH ON A STICK

Sticking with food that can be enjoyed while walking around your favorite festival or as you trek from one daily commission to the next, this recipe highlights the delicious yet subtle flavor of radishes. Don't forget to season properly and eat these while they're hot!

1. Using a vegetable peeler, remove the skin from the radish. Then use a grater to shred the radish into a large bowl.

2. Sprinkle the grated radish with a pinch of salt and let sit for a few minutes to draw out the water from the radish. Drain the excess water and use a paper towel to squeeze out any remaining water from the radish.

3. Add the eggs, flour, green onion, vegetable stock, ginger, and remaining seasonings. Mix well.

4. Shape the radish mixture into balls. (The smaller the balls, the faster they will cook.)

5. Add vegetable oil to a skillet over medium heat. Gently place the radish balls in the oil and fry all together for 5 minutes or until golden brown, turning them occasionally to ensure all sides are frying evenly. Serve with an aioli or your favorite sauce.

SERVES: 4 | **PREP TIME:** 10 minutes | **COOK TIME:** 20 minutes

20 raw shrimp

3 medium russet potatoes, peeled and cut into 1-inch cubes

1 tablespoon unsalted butter

1 egg yolk + 1 large egg, divided

pinch + 1½ teaspoons salt, divided

pinch + 1 teaspoon pepper, divided

2 teaspoons paprika

¼ teaspoon dried thyme

2 teaspoons garlic powder

1 cup all-purpose flour + 2 tablespoons, if needed

1 cup panko bread crumbs

vegetable oil, for frying

CRISPY POTATO-SHRIMP BALLS

If you feel as if your health has hit rock bottom, nothing will heal you faster than a delicious plate of Crispy Potato-Shrimp Balls. These cute and compact balls of fried goodness make this dish the perfect appetizer for your next gathering with friends!

1. Peel off the shrimp shells, leaving the tails on. Season with a pinch of salt and pepper and set aside.

2. Boil the potatoes in water over medium-high heat for 15 to 20 minutes, or until fork tender. Mash them using a potato masher, then add in the unsalted butter and egg yolk. Mix until smooth. Your potatoes should be creamy but not soupy. If they are too soupy, add a little flour until the potatoes are thickened to a creamy texture.

3. Add the 1½ teaspoons salt, 1 teaspoon pepper, paprika, thyme, and garlic powder. Mix well.

4. Scoop out ⅓ cup of the potato mixture and use your hands to form it into a ball. Using your thumb, poke a hole in the top of the ball, place a shrimp in the hole, then cover the shrimp with the potatoes until just the shrimp tail is sticking out. Squeeze slightly to tighten everything and make sure the shrimp stays locked inside.

5. Pour 1 cup flour into a shallow dish. Then crack the egg into a separate dish and whisk to combine the yolk and egg white. Add the panko crumbs to another shallow dish.

6. Carefully roll a potato-shrimp ball into the flour, shaking off any excess. Then roll in the egg wash and then the bread crumbs. Make sure the ball is fully covered with all three ingredients. Set aside on a large plate or tray and repeat for the remaining potato-shrimp balls.

7. Fill a medium frying pan halfway with vegetable oil and heat to between 350°F to 375°F over medium heat. Fry the shrimp balls together until the outside is golden brown, about 4 minutes, turning occasionally to ensure all shrimp balls are frying evenly.

8. Remove from the oil and let the potato-shrimp balls cool for a few minutes. Enjoy by themselves or serve with an aioli or your favorite sauce.

✦ ✦ ✦

SERVES: 4 | **PREP TIME:** 15 minutes | **COOK TIME:** 20 minutes

1 package prosciutto
(9 to 12 slices)

7 slices deli ham

2 links cured chorizo,
salami, or kielbasa

cherry tomatoes,
for serving

lettuce leaves, for serving

CLASSIC COLD CUTS

If you're looking for the perfect snack between meals or a light appetizer before your next dinner party, a platter of delicious meats is the way to go. Eat each slice by itself or gather a few to make a mini sandwich—either way, you'll feel ready to tackle whatever quest (or meal) comes next!

1. On a flat platter or board, arrange the prosciutto slices as light and airy ribbons covering a third of the serving plate.

2. On another third of the platter, fan the ham pieces out like a deck of cards, or fold each piece in half twice so they are easy to grab.

3. Cut the sausages into round slices and arrange on the last third of the platter.

4. Place some cherry tomatoes and a few leaves of lettuce in the middle of the platter. You can also tuck a few lettuce leaves under the meat slices and along the edge of the platter.

✦ ✦ ✦

SERVES: 4 | **PREP TIME:** 10 minutes

8 eggs

3½ tablespoons water

1 tablespoon soy sauce

¾ teaspoon sugar

1 tablespoon olive oil

SPECIAL EQUIPMENT
tamagoyaki pan (optional)

ELEGANT EGG ROLL

While this dish looks simple enough, there's an art to mixing the eggs to fluffy perfection and rolling them into a rectangular loaf. You may need to practice a bit before you're ready to serve this dish to others.

1. In a medium bowl, combine the eggs, water, soy sauce, and sugar. Using a whisk, beat until well combined.

2. Heat a tamagoyaki pan (rectangular Japanese omelet pan) or a small frying pan over medium heat. Using a pastry brush, lightly coat the bottom of the pan with olive oil.

3. Pour a thin layer of the egg mixture to cover the surface of the pan. When it's about 80 percent cooked but still wet on the surface, use chopsticks or wooden tongs to start gently rolling in the edges to form a rolled omelet. Move the rolled omelet to one side of the pan.

4. Brush the pan with oil again and pour in another thin layer of the egg mixture. Using a spoon, gently lift the previously made omelet and spread some of the uncooked egg mixture underneath. This will help both omelets stick together. When this next layer of eggs is 80 percent cooked but the surface is still wet, start with the previously made omelet and gently roll it up with the new layer. Set to one side of the pan. Repeat this process until the egg mixture is gone. Your omelet will have 3 to 4 layers.

5. Transfer the rolled omelet onto a cutting board and allow to rest for several minutes. Cut into even 2-inch slices and serve.

SERVES: 2 | **PREP TIME:** 5 minutes | **COOK TIME:** 10 minutes

MISO SOUP

FOR THE DASHI BROTH:

4 cups water

1½ pieces (about 0.45 ounce) kombu (dried kelp)

1 cup katsuobushi (dried bonito flakes)

FOR THE MISO SOUP:

4 to 5 tablespoons dark miso (1 tablespoon for every cup of dashi)

1 (8-ounce) package silken tofu, cut into ½-inch cubes

1 tablespoon dried wakame seaweed

1 teaspoon sesame oil

2 green onions, thinly sliced

TIP: You may not have many of the ingredients needed for this recipe just sitting in your pantry, and they might be difficult to find at your grocery store. To find things like kombu, bonito flakes, and wakame seaweed, head to your local Asian market or an Asian grocery store like H Mart. There are also lots of online grocery shopping apps these days, such as Weee! and Umamicart, that are specifically for buying Asian ingredients.

Is there anything better than a side of miso soup? Whether you make it for breakfast, lunch, or dinner, the salty and savory flavors of this dish will ensure that you have all the energy you need to farm for materials or begin a new quest.

1. To make the dashi broth, combine the water and kombu in a medium saucepan. Heat over medium-low heat for about 15 minutes, or until the water is just about to boil. This will extract all the umami flavor from the kombu. Remove the kombu and discard, or set aside for a different recipe. (Yes, you can reuse it!)

2. Add the katsuobushi to the saucepan and bring to a boil over medium heat. Once boiling, reduce the heat and simmer the dashi for 30 seconds more.

3. Remove the dashi from the heat and let it rest for about 10 minutes. This should give the bonito flakes time to sink to the bottom of the pan. Then strain the dashi through a fine-mesh sieve into a bowl to remove the bonito flakes.

4. To make the miso soup, pour the strained dashi back into the saucepan. Put the miso in a ladle or large spoon and dip into the dashi. Stir until the miso dissolves completely.

5. Add the tofu, then gently stir in the dried wakame seaweed and sesame oil. Heat the miso soup on medium-low heat for 5 minutes, or until warm. Be careful not to boil (boiled miso soup loses both flavor and nutrients).

6. Pour into a soup bowl and top with green onion slices to serve.

SERVES: 4 | **PREP TIME:** 10 minutes + 10 minutes resting time | **COOK TIME:** 20 minutes

4 ounces dried matsutake mushrooms

3 tablespoons all-purpose flour

2 tablespoons salted butter

1 teaspoon vegetable oil

pepper, to taste

Butter-Sautéed Mushrooms

Foraging is a skill every adventurer should master. However, if you're just starting out and have only been able to gather a few mushrooms here and there, this recipe will help you turn them into a tasty dish that even the most experienced forager would be proud of. Butter-Sautéed Mushrooms can be the perfect side dish for Sweet Roasted Chicken (page 80), Smoked Chicken from the North (page 90), Grilled Steak (page 99), and more!

1. Soak the mushrooms in warm water for 30 minutes. Then drain well and pat dry with a paper towel.
2. Place the flour in a shallow dish and dip each mushroom into it to coat both sides. Shake off the excess.
3. Add the butter and oil to a nonstick frying pan over medium-high heat. When the butter is melted, add the mushrooms and season with black pepper. Cook for 10 minutes, flipping the mushrooms halfway through.
4. Sprinkle with extra pepper if desired. Serve immediately.

✦ ✦ ✦

SERVES: 2 | **PREP TIME:** 5 minutes + 30 minutes soaking time | **COOK TIME:** 12 minutes

LOADED BAKED POTATO

3 large baking potatoes (about 1 pound each)

1 teaspoon olive oil

4 tablespoons (½ stick) unsalted butter, cut into cubes

½ cup chopped green onions + more, for serving

4 to 5 cremini mushrooms, chopped

½ cup half-and-half

½ cup sour cream

salt and pepper, to taste

1 cup shredded cheddar cheesew

This Loaded Baked Potato is one of the most versatile side dishes you can make. Pair it with Sweet Roasted Chicken (page 80), Honey-Glazed Roast (page 96), or Grilled Steak (page 99) for a complete and hearty dinner sure to impress old friends and new travel companions alike. And if you happen to run into a quirky group of gourmets during your adventures, take a cue from them and don't be afraid to mix and match toppings to create a delicious, one-of-a-kind baked potato side dish!

1. Preheat the oven to 400°F. Pierce the potatoes several times with a fork and rub with olive oil. Bake until tender, 50 to 75 minutes. While baking, you can check if the potatoes are done by sticking a skewer or a fork into them; if soft, they are ready.

2. Remove the potatoes from the oven. When cool enough to handle, slice the top off each potato horizontally (about 1 inch). Scoop out the potato pulp and transfer it to a large mixing bowl, leaving thin potato shells. Set the potato skins aside and reduce the oven temperature to 375°F.

3. In a small skillet, melt the butter over medium-high heat, then add the onions and mushrooms and sauté until tender, about 5 minutes.

4. In the mixing bowl, using a potato masher, mash the potato pulp. Stir in the sautéed onions and mushrooms, half-and-half, sour cream, salt, and pepper. Stuff this mixture into the 3 potato shells and top with cheddar cheese.

5. Place the stuffed potatoes on a baking sheet and bake until heated through, about 20 minutes. Top with extra chopped green onions to serve.

✦ ✦ ✦

SERVES: 3 | **PREP TIME:** 10 minutes | **COOK TIME:** 1 hour 10 minutes to 1 hour 35 minutes

FOR THE MASHED POTATOES:

6 medium Yukon Gold potatoes

1 cup half-and-half

½ cup (1 stick) unsalted butter, at room temperature

½ cup sour cream

salt and pepper, to taste

FOR THE GRAVY:

2 cups beef stock or broth

2 beef bouillon cubes

2 tablespoons unsalted butter

¼ cup all-purpose flour

¼ teaspoon dried thyme

¼ teaspoon dried parsley

½ teaspoon dried sage

½ teaspoon onion powder

2 tablespoons soy sauce

2 tablespoons Worcestershire sauce

salt and pepper, to taste

RICH MASHED POTATOES

Perfectly seasoned and smooth as butter, these mashed potatoes will make you question whether you really created a dish as rich as this from a few humble potatoes. The gravy offers another irresistible layer of flavor.

1. Peel the potatoes and cut them into small, bite-size chunks. Place in a large stockpot and add water so the potatoes are just covered. Bring the water to a boil over high heat, then reduce the heat to medium and simmer for 8 to 10 minutes, until the potatoes are fork tender.

2. Drain the water from the pot. Using a potato masher, mash the potatoes for 2 to 3 minutes to release the heat and steam.

3. Add the half-and-half, stick of butter, sour cream, salt, and pepper. Continue mashing for another minute, until the potatoes are silky and smooth.

4. Transfer the potatoes to a serving dish and keep warm by covering with foil and placing in the oven on low.

5. To make the gravy, add the stock or broth to a medium saucepan over medium-low heat and crumble in the bouillon cubes. Heat for 1 to 2 minutes, stirring constantly, until the bouillon is fully dissolved. Pour into a bowl and set aside.

6. In the same saucepan over medium heat, melt the 2 tablespoons butter. Add the flour and spices and cook for 1 minute, stirring constantly. Then slowly whisk in the stock until all the flour lumps are dissolved and the mixture is smooth. Stir in the soy sauce and Worcestershire sauce. Bring to a boil, then immediately reduce the heat to a simmer. Continue whisking until the gravy reaches the desired smoothness and thickness, about 1 minute.

7. Remove gravy from the heat and season with salt and pepper. Pour gently over the mashed potatoes and serve!

SERVES: 5 | **PREP TIME:** 10 minutes | **COOK TIME:** 15 minutes

1 cup milk, heated to 110°F

1 teaspoon active dry yeast

3 tablespoons sugar

2¾ cups all-purpose flour + extra, for rolling

½ teaspoon salt

1 tablespoon olive oil

1 teaspoon white vinegar

SPECIAL EQUIPMENT

stand mixer with dough hook

steamer

STEAMED BUNS

This humble dish is a staple for most people you'll meet on your travels. Whether you've just finished mining some ore for the local blacksmith or cleared out the nearby enemy camp, these Steamed Buns always taste better after a hard day's work.

1. In a small bowl, combine the heated milk, yeast, and sugar. Stir with chopsticks or a wooden spoon and cover with plastic wrap. Set aside for 10 minutes.

2. After the milk mixture has rested, pour it into the bowl of a stand mixer with dough hook attached. Add the 2¾ cups flour and ½ teaspoon salt and mix on low speed until a smooth dough is formed, about 10 minutes.

3. Brush a large mixing bowl with olive oil. Transfer the dough into the oiled bowl, cover with plastic wrap, and let rest for 15 minutes.

4. On a lightly floured surface, use a rolling pin to roll the dough into a 14 x 10-inch rectangle. Then use your hands to roll it into a tight 10-inch log.

5. Gently roll out the dough log into another flat rectangle, and then reroll it into a log. Do this a few times, until the surface of the dough looks smooth. Finish by rolling the dough into a 12-inch log. Cut the dough log into 8 equal-sized pieces and use your hands to gently roll these pieces into round balls. Transfer each bun to a paper cupcake liner.

6. Place the buns in a steamer, leaving a bit of space between them. Cover the steamer and let the buns rise for 50 minutes, or until doubled in size.

7. Add enough water mixed with 1 teaspoon of white vinegar to the bottom of the steamer until the water rests about 1 inch under the steamer. Cover with the lid.

8. Turn on high heat and steam for 10 to 12 minutes, or until the dough expands to form soft and fluffy steamed buns. Turn off the heat and let the buns sit in the steamer for 3 more minutes to prevent them from wrinkling from temperature shock. Serve warm.

◆ ◆ ◆

SERVES: 4 | **PREP TIME:** 40 minutes + 50 minutes for dough rising | **COOK TIME:** 13 to 15 minutes + 50 minutes for dough rising

FOR THE BUNS:

1 cup corn flour + extra, if needed

1 cup sticky (glutinous) rice flour (or regular rice flour or all-purpose flour)

1 tablespoon sugar

1 cup warm water

oil, for brushing steamer

FOR THE PORK FILLING:

1 tablespoon vegetable oil

1 cup (½ pound) ground pork

½ teaspoon onion powder

½ teaspoon chili powder, or to taste

1 teaspoon smoked or regular paprika

2 cloves garlic, minced

½ teaspoon ground cumin

salt and pepper, to taste

¼ cup tomato puree

1 green onion, sliced, for serving

1 chili pepper, sliced, for serving

SPECIAL EQUIPMENT
steamer

Spicy Cornbread Buns

These aren't your average buns. Instead of being stuffed with a savory filling and then cooked, these Spicy Cornbread Buns are cooked separately from the filling so that you can dip them in and eat as much or as little of the filling as you want. When eaten together, the soft dough of the buns and the fragrant mixture of pork and spices create a culinary adventure in your mouth. While you may want to hoard this delicious snack for yourself, this is the perfect dish to bring to your next gathering of friends.

1. To make the buns, in a large bowl, combine the corn flour, sticky rice flour, and sugar. Mix well and add the warm water. Using your hands, knead for about 3 minutes to form a dough. Add more corn flour if the dough seems too wet to shape.

2. Roll the dough into a log and cut into 7 even pieces.

3. Brush a bamboo steamer or a steam rack with oil.

4. Form a piece of dough into a ball. Then wet your hand and use your thumb to make a hole in the ball, forming a cone-shaped bun with a hollow inside. Do the same with all the dough pieces. Place on the oiled steamer.

5. Boil water in a large pot over medium heat, making sure it doesn't come high enough in the pot to touch the steamer. Place the steamer over the pot of water.

6. Cover with the lid wrapped in a kitchen towel (to prevent any water droplets from falling onto the buns) and steam for 20 minutes. Then turn off the heat and leave covered for 5 more minutes.

7. While the buns are steaming, start making the spicy meat dip. Add the 1 tablespoon oil and ground pork to a large frying pan over medium-high heat. Using a spatula or a large wooden spoon, break the meat apart and cook until browned, about 5 minutes. Stir in the onion powder, chili powder, paprika, minced garlic, cumin, salt, and pepper. Cook until fragrant, about 30 seconds, stirring frequently.

8. Add the tomato puree and cook for 5 more minutes, or until the liquid is reduced.

9. Transfer the spicy meat dip sauce to the middle of a serving plate. Sprinkle with sliced green onion and top with the sliced chili pepper. Arrange the buns around the meat dip and serve immediately.

✦ ✦ ✦

SERVES: 4 | **PREP TIME:** 10 minutes | **COOK TIME:** 35 minutes

FOR THE MASALA PASTE:

1 large red onion

3 large cloves garlic

2 tablespoons minced fresh ginger

3 tablespoons garam masala

2¼ teaspoons chili powder

2 tablespoons minced fresh turmeric or ground turmeric

1 tablespoon ground cumin

1 tablespoon ground coriander

½ teaspoon ground cinnamon

½ teaspoon ground cloves

2 teaspoons salt

½ teaspoon cayenne pepper

½ cup shelled almonds

handful of cilantro stems

juice of 2 limes

FOR THE MASALA SAUCE:

2 tablespoons olive oil

1 (12-ounce) can tomato puree

½ cup water or vegetable broth

1 (13.5-ounce) can coconut milk

½ teaspoon salt, or to taste

CHEESY MASALA BITES

A favorite of certain forest-dwelling creatures, this dish brings together some of the best ingredients you can find—cheese, potatoes, and an amazing mix of spices. Combine everything, fry it up, and you've got a dish that will keep you satisfied through hours of adventuring.

1. Pulse all the ingredients for the masala paste together in a food processor until smooth.

2. To make the masala sauce, transfer ¼ cup of the paste to a medium pot along with 2 tablespoons olive oil. (Reserve the rest of the paste to use in other recipes.)

3. Cook over medium heat, stirring frequently, until fragrant, about 3 minutes. Add the tomato puree and water or broth and simmer for 10 minutes. Stir in the coconut milk and ½ teaspoon salt, and simmer for 10 more minutes, until thick and creamy. Set aside while you prepare the cheese bites.

4. To make the cheese bites, cook the cubed potatoes in a pot of boiling water for 15 minutes, or until fork tender. Drain and mash in the pot until smooth using a potato masher. Make sure there are no lumps.

5. Add the garlic powder, chili powder, pinch of salt and pepper, thyme, 6 tablespoons bread crumbs, and mint. Mix well. Divide the mixture into 10 equal sized balls and place on a plate. Cover and set aside.

6. Cut the mozzarella cheese into ½-inch cubes. In a small bowl, mix together the oregano, allspice, and ⅛ teaspoon pepper. Toss the cheese cubes in this mixture and set aside.

7. In the palm of your hand, spread a potato ball evenly into a small patty. Place a cheese cube in the center and gently bring the edges together to reform the ball around the cheese. Make sure the ball is sealed well, without any cracks. Set aside on a plate. Repeat for the remaining cheese bites.

FOR THE CHEESE BITES:

3 or 4 medium russet or Yukon Gold potatoes, peeled and cubed

1 teaspoon garlic powder

½ teaspoon chili powder, or to taste

pinch of salt

pinch of black pepper + ⅛ teaspoon, divided

½ teaspoon dried thyme

6 tablespoons bread crumbs + ½ cup, divided

2 tablespoons finely chopped fresh mint + extra, for serving

3½ ounces mozzarella cheese

½ teaspoon dried oregano

⅛ teaspoon ground allspice

2 tablespoons corn flour

1 egg, beaten

vegetable oil, for frying

8. Place the 2 tablespoons corn flour in a shallow bowl, the beaten egg in another bowl, and ½ cup bread crumbs in a third bowl. Roll each cheese bite first in the corn flour, then in the beaten egg, and then in the bread crumbs. Return the coated cheese bites to the plate.

9. In a wide, deep skillet over medium heat, pour just enough oil to immerse all of the cheese bites halfway. Before frying, drop a small piece of the potato mixture into the oil to test if it's ready. When it's at the right temperature, the potato mixture will float to the surface immediately without browning.

10. Gently place the cheese bites one by one into the oil and leave them for 1 to 2 minutes. Then gently stir them and fry for 5 more minutes, or until golden and crisp.

11. Pour masala sauce into individual serving bowls and top with cheese bites. Decorate with fresh mint to serve.

✦ ✦ ✦

SERVES: 3 | **PREP TIME:** 20 minutes | **COOK TIME:** 40 minutes

BREAKFAST

2 cups all-purpose flour

¼ cup granulated sugar

4 teaspoons baking powder

¼ teaspoon baking soda

½ teaspoon salt

1¾ cups whole milk

4 tablespoons (½ stick) unsalted butter, melted + more, for frying

2 teaspoons pure vanilla extract

1 egg

honey or maple syrup, for serving

golden-colored berry, such as a golden raspberry or white currant (optional)

AFTERNOON TEA PANCAKES

When you're done fighting your way through the latest domain or have finally finished that side quest you've been putting off for weeks (okay, months), it may be a good idea to recover your strength with a stack of the fluffiest pancakes ever. While Afternoon Tea Pancakes make the perfect breakfast for your average adventurer, they are often served with a spot of afternoon tea at the larger estates in town (hence the fancy golden berries on top). So not only will you feel newly energized once you've eaten them, but you'll get a taste for how the wealthier citizens live.

1. In a large mixing bowl, combine the flour, sugar, baking powder, baking soda, and salt. Mix thoroughly, using a wire whisk.

2. Make a well in the center of your dry ingredients and add the milk, butter, vanilla, and egg. Whisk the wet ingredients together in the well first before slowly folding them into the dry ingredients. Combine until smooth.

3. Heat a nonstick pan over medium-low heat and add a small dollop of butter to lightly grease the pan.

4. Using a ladle, pour about ¼ cup of batter onto the pan and gently spread with the back of the ladle to create a round shape.

5. Cook until bubbles begin to appear on the surface of the pancake and the underside is golden, about 4 minutes. Then flip with a spatula and cook until the other side is golden. Repeat with the remaining batter.

6. Drizzle with honey or maple syrup and decorate with a golden-colored berry on top, if you wish.

◆ ◆ ◆

SERVES: 3 | **PREP TIME:** 5 minutes | **COOK TIME:** 20 minutes

FOR THE HOLLANDAISE SAUCE:

4 tablespoons (½ stick) unsalted butter

4 egg yolks

1 tablespoon lemon juice

1 teaspoon Dijon mustard

1 tablespoon heavy cream, or more, as needed

salt and pepper, to taste

pinch of cayenne pepper

FOR THE BREAKFAST SANDWICHES:

4 eggs

splash of white vinegar

4 thick-cut ham slices

2 English muffins

salt and pepper, to taste

smoked paprika, to taste

1 green onion, chopped, for serving

BREAKFAST OF ADVENTURERS

If your adventure party eats this dish for breakfast, there's no obstacle you won't be able to overcome in the day ahead! The creaminess of the sauce and the yoke of the poached egg cut through the saltiness of the ham to make a dish that is hard to beat in terms of flavor, texture, and aesthetics. And if you're looking for a little more sustenance to fill your stomachs before your next adventure, pair this dish with some Afternoon Tea Pancakes (page 39) and Crispy Baked Hash Browns (page 47) for a full breakfast spread.

1. To make the hollandaise sauce, melt the butter in a small saucepan over medium-low heat.

2. While the butter is melting, use a wire whisk to beat the egg yolks in a medium bowl. Add the remaining ingredients for the hollandaise sauce to the beaten egg yolks and mix until thoroughly combined.

3. Add a small spoonful of the melted butter to the hollandaise sauce and stir to blend. Repeat this process, adding a small spoonful at a time, until all the butter has been incorporated into the sauce.

4. Now pour the sauce into the saucepan used for the butter, reduce the heat to low, and stir constantly for about 30 seconds. Remove from the heat and let the sauce thicken, about 5 minutes, then stir. If the consistency is too thick, thin with a small splash of the cream. Set the sauce aside while you poach the eggs.

5. To poach the eggs, bring 3 inches of water to a boil in a medium pot. Then reduce the heat to a simmer and add a splash of white vinegar. Crack an egg into a shallow bowl or cup and slowly lower to just above the simmering water, then gently tip so the egg slides into the water.

6. Let the egg cook for 3 minutes if you want runny yolks, 4 minutes if you want medium yolks, and 5 minutes if you want hard yolks. Use a slotted spoon to remove the poached egg from the water. Repeat with remaining eggs.

7. While the eggs are cooking, place the ham slices in a medium frying pan over medium heat and brown for 1 minute on each side. Toast the English muffins in a toaster or by lightly frying them next to your ham slices.

8. To assemble the sandwiches, place the two halves of each toasted English muffin on separate plates, then top each half with a slice of ham. Carefully place the poached eggs on the ham and pour the hollandaise sauce over the top. Sprinkle with salt, pepper, smoked paprika, and chopped green onion.

◆ ◆ ◆

SERVES: 2 | **PREP TIME:** 10 minutes | **COOK TIME:** 25 minutes

FOR THE BREAD:

4 cups strong white bread flour (or all-purpose flour) + more, for flouring work surface

1 teaspoon salt

1 packet (¼ ounce) fast action dried yeast

2 tablespoons olive oil + more, for oiling bowl and pan

1 cup + 3 to 4 tablespoons water

FOR THE TOPPING:

2 Roma tomatoes, cut into chunks

2 tablespoons olive oil

splash of water

salt and pepper, to taste

½ red onion, sliced

whole parsley leaves, for serving

SPECIAL EQUIPMENT

stand mixer with dough hook

standard-size loaf pan

INVIGORATING MORNING TOAST

From fishermen to shop owners to innkeepers, early risers everywhere need something to wake them up (and keep them up!) and get them ready for a day of rewarding work. This toast makes the perfect breakfast—if the unexpected combination of creamy tomato sauce and onions on toast doesn't shock you awake, the onion breath you get by eating it probably will!

1. To make the bread, in the bowl of a stand mixer, combine the flour, salt, and yeast, mixing gently with a spoon or spatula.

2. Mix in the 2 tablespoons olive oil and then add water. Different flours have different levels of absorbency, so start by adding 1 cup plus 3 tablespoons and mix together to form a rough dough. If it's too dry, you can add more water, but you shouldn't need more than 1¼ cups in all.

3. Attach the dough hook, set the mixer on low speed, and knead the dough for 10 minutes.

4. Lightly oil a large bowl and place the dough in it. Cover with plastic wrap and leave in a warm place to rise for 1 hour, or until doubled in size.

5. Tip the dough out onto a floured work surface and use your hands to flatten it into a rectangle roughly as wide as the length of the loaf pan and about ½ to 1 inch thick.

6. Roll the dough up from one of the short ends, using your thumbs to keep the roll tight and press the dough together. Once it's rolled into a log, use your fingers to pinch the seam together.

7. Turn the dough over so the seam is on the bottom. Lightly oil your loaf pan, then transfer the dough into the pan. Loosely cover with plastic wrap and leave to rise for 30 minutes.

8. Preheat the oven to 425° F. Remove the plastic wrap and bake the dough for 30 minutes, or until golden and risen and the bread sounds hollow when the top is tapped. Allow to cool in the pan fully before slicing.

9. To make the topping, place the sliced tomatoes and the olive oil in a pan over medium-high heat. Cook for 3 minutes, stirring occasionally, and then add a splash of water, salt, and pepper to taste. Cover and cook, stirring occasionally, until the tomato slices are soft and the water is turning into a thick sauce.

10. To serve, cut 4 thick slices of the bread and top with the cooked tomatoes. Add sliced red onion and parsley leaf and sprinkle with extra pepper.

✦ ✦ ✦

SERVES: 4 | **PREP TIME:** 20 minutes + 1½ hours rising time | **COOK TIME:** 40 minutes

CRISPY BAKED HASH BROWNS

1 (30-ounce) package frozen shredded hash brown potatoes, thawed

2 eggs

1 cup shredded cheddar cheese

salt and pepper, to taste

1 teaspoon ground cumin

1 teaspoon dried mint

½ teaspoon garlic powder

½ teaspoon onion powder

½ cup (1 stick) unsalted butter, melted

While experienced Travelers have learned to coat potatoes in finely ground pine cones before frying them up into delicious hash browns, I recommend leaving the pine cones to the professionals. Your typical all-purpose flour will see you through in this recipe. Pair your Crispy Baked Hash Browns with a Fried Egg (page 48) for a classic breakfast duo that delivers on taste and will fuel you up for your travels.

1. Preheat the oven to 400°F. Line a baking sheet with parchment paper and set aside.

2. Pour the shredded potatoes into a large bowl. In a small separate bowl, whisk the eggs. Add the eggs to the potatoes along with the shredded cheese and all the seasonings. Toss to coat everything evenly. Pour the melted butter over the top and toss once again to coat.

3. Spread the potato mixture evenly over the parchment-lined baking sheet. Bake for 40 minutes, or until the potatoes turn a light golden-brown color.

4. Remove from the oven. Using a round cookie cutter, cut the potatoes into individual hash brown circles to serve.

◆ ◆ ◆

SERVES: 4 | **PREP TIME:** 10 minutes | **COOK TIME:** 40 minutes

FRIED EGG

1 teaspoon unsalted butter

1 teaspoon vegetable oil

2 eggs, as fresh as possible

salt, to taste

freshly-ground black pepper, to taste

green onion sliced, for serving

Making the perfect sunny-side-up egg is practically an art form all its own. It requires concentration and great observational skills—both qualities that mark a talented adventurer. But if luck isn't on your side while making this dish, a little char around the edges only adds a bit more flavor. Whip up a Fried Egg or two with some Crispy Baked Hash Browns (page 47) for a hearty breakfast that you just can't say no to.

1. In a large nonstick skillet, heat the butter and oil over medium-low heat.
2. When the butter is melted, crack the eggs into the skillet and sprinkle with a pinch of salt and a few grinds of pepper.
3. Cook for 2 to 3 minutes, or until the egg white is firm but the yolk is still runny. Do not flip.
4. Transfer to a serving plate, sprinkle with green onion, and dig in!

✦ ✦ ✦

SERVES: 1 | **PREP TIME:** 1 minute | **COOK TIME:** 2 to 3 minutes

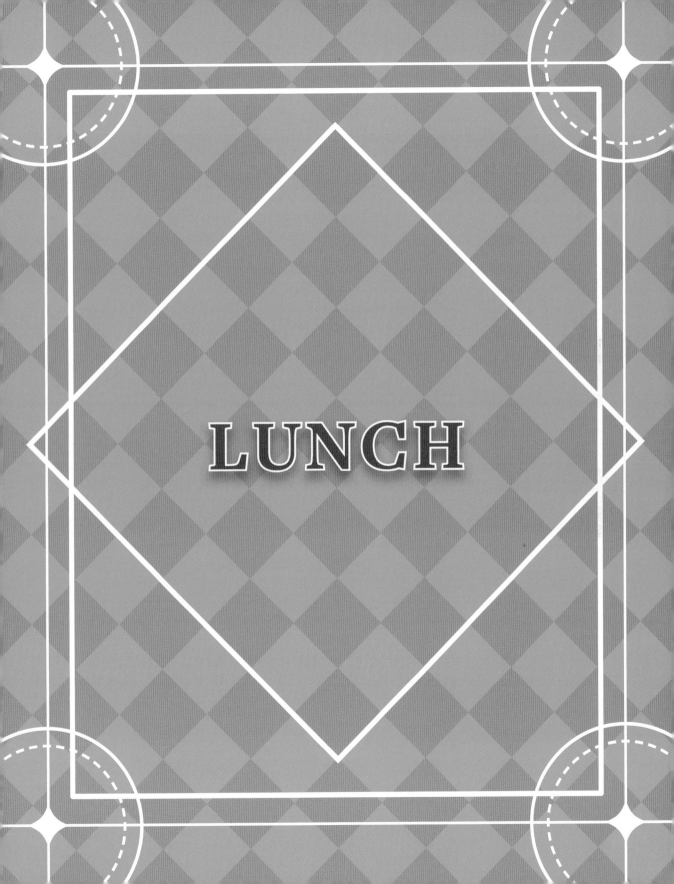

LUNCH

WHITE SAUCE STEW

1 tablespoon
unsalted butter

1 tablespoon vegetable oil

1 onion, chopped

1 pound lean chuck
steak (or similar cut),
cut into chunks

2 cloves garlic, minced

½ cup dry white wine

4 cups beef stock

3 large carrots, peeled

4 medium potatoes, skin on

1 bay leaf

1 teaspoon fresh
thyme, chopped

1 cup water + 3
tablespoons, divided

3 tablespoons cornstarch

¼ cup heavy cream

½ teaspoon pepper
+ more, to taste

salt, to taste

There's nothing like a hearty stew to keep your energy level high and help you stay sharp for your next quest. This classic stew is easy to make on the road yet doesn't skip out on flavor—perfect for new and seasoned adventurers alike.

1. In a large pot, combine the butter, oil, and onion. Sauté over medium-high heat for 5 minutes, or until the onion pieces are translucent.

2. Add the beef chunks and sear on all sides. Add the minced garlic and cook for 30 seconds, stirring frequently.

3. Pour in the white wine and cook for about 5 minutes, or until the liquid is evaporated. Add the beef stock and ½ teaspoon pepper. Stir well and bring to a boil. Then reduce the heat to low, cover the pot with a lid, and simmer for 2 hours, stirring occasionally, until the beef is fork tender.

4. Just before the beef is done simmering, roughly chop the carrots and potatoes and add to the pot. Add the bay leaf, thyme, and 1 cup water. Increase the heat to medium and cook for at least 20 to 30 more minutes, until the veggies are tender.

5. Mix the cornstarch and 3 tablespoons water in a small bowl to create a slurry. Pour into the pot and stir while cooking over medium heat until the stew thickens to a gravy-like consistency.

6. Remove the stew from the heat and pour in the cream, stirring well. Add salt and pepper to taste and ladle into bowls to serve.

✦ ✦ ✦

SERVES: 4 | **PREP TIME:** 10 minutes | **COOK TIME:** 2½ hours

RADISH SOUP

3 tablespoons olive oil + more, for broiling the tomatoes

1 carrot, chopped into ½-inch pieces

1 stalk celery, chopped into ½-inch pieces

1 onion, chopped into ½-inch pieces

5 cloves garlic, minced

1 tablespoon chopped fresh mint + more, for serving

1 tablespoon paprika

2 cups canned crushed tomatoes

1 medium daikon radish, half chopped and half sliced in rounds

8 cups vegetable stock

salt and pepper, to taste

2 Roma tomatoes, sliced

SPECIAL EQUIPMENT
immersion blender

If you're looking for the perfect summertime soup, look no further. Radishes make for a light and flavorful broth that will fill you up and keep you thinking about dandelion seeds drifting in a soft summer breeze, and sharing a meal with friends in the shade of a tall tree—all the very best parts of summer.

1. In a large pot over medium-high heat, combine the oil, carrots, celery, and onion and cook for 5 minutes, or until the onion turns translucent.

2. Add the garlic and 1 tablespoon mint and sauté for 1 minute, stirring frequently. Then stir in the paprika and sauté for 2 more minutes.

3. Add the crushed tomatoes, chopped daikon, and vegetable stock. Stir well and bring to a boil. Add salt and pepper to taste. Then lower heat to medium and let simmer uncovered for 30 minutes.

4. Turn on the oven broiler to 500°F.

5. Slice the tomatoes and place them on a sheet pan. Drizzle with olive oil and sprinkle with salt and pepper. Broil for 5 minutes.

6. Using an immersion blender, puree the soup until the desired consistency is reached. Ladle into bowls and top with the broiled tomato slices and sliced radish rounds. Sprinkle on fresh mint to serve.

❖ ❖ ❖

SERVES: 4 | **PREP TIME:** 10 minutes | **COOK TIME:** 45 minutes

18 ounces (5 to 6 heads) baby bok choy

2 tablespoons toasted sesame oil

3 large garlic cloves, sliced

1 teaspoon minced fresh ginger

pinch of salt

1 (16-ounce) tofu block, cut into cubes

3½ cups vegetable stock

3 tablespoons soy sauce

3 egg yolks

2 green onions, sliced, for serving

sesame seeds, for serving

chili pepper, sliced, for serving

PEARL AND JADE SOUP

Cubes of fresh white tofu and slices of vibrant green bok choy become jewel-like delicacies when glistening in a light broth. Pearl and Jade Soup is one of those modest recipes that feel and taste like the most luxurious dish.

1. Slice the bok choy heads in half lengthwise. For large bundles, quarter them.

2. Preheat a medium soup pot over medium-low heat until it feels warm. Add the sesame oil, garlic, ginger, and pinch of salt. Raise the heat to medium and sauté until fragrant, about 1 minute.

3. Add the tofu cubes and vegetable stock and cover with a lid; bring to a boil over medium-high heat, about 4 minutes. Then lower the heat to low and simmer for 5 minutes.

4. Add the soy sauce. Raise the heat to medium and add the bok choy. Cook for 1 to 2 minutes, uncovered, then turn off the heat.

5. Whisk the egg yolks in a small bowl, adding a few splashes of the soup while whisking. Then pour the mixture into the soup and stir.

6. Divide the soup into 4 serving bowls and sprinkle green onion slices, sesame seeds, and sliced chili pepper on top.

SERVES: 2 | **PREP TIME:** 10 minutes | **COOK TIME:** 15 minutes

Ingredients

½ teaspoon salt + more, to taste

¼ teaspoon black pepper

2 tablespoons Shaoxing cooking wine (or dry sherry), divided

1 egg white

1½ tablespoons potato starch

1 tablespoon vegetable oil

1 pound white fish fillets (such as perch, tilapia, or catfish), cut into ½-inch slices

3 cups vegetable stock

2 cups water

4 cloves garlic, thinly sliced

6 slices fresh ginger

3 green onions, sliced + 1 green onion, chopped, for serving

1 cup bean sprouts, fresh or canned

½ cup olive oil

1 tablespoon smoked paprika

1 tablespoon dried red chili peppers

½ tablespoon red Sichuan peppercorns, crushed or ground

red bell pepper, sliced, for serving

SPICY FISH STEW

Impress your local famous opera singer by making her favorite dish: Spicy Fish Stew. The chili peppers give the broth a great kick, pairing perfectly with the subtle, fresh fish flavor. It's best eaten on a cold day, whether you're huddled by a campfire on your travels or at home surrounded by friends.

1. Start by making a marinade for the fish. In a large bowl, combine ½ teaspoon salt, the black pepper, and 1 tablespoon Shaoxing wine; mix well. Add the egg white and potato starch, mixing once more. Pour in 1 tablespoon vegetable oil, then add the fish. Cover and let marinate in the refrigerator for at least 30 minutes.

2. In a wok or large saucepan over high heat, combine the vegetable stock, water, garlic, ginger, 3 sliced green onions, and remaining Shaoxing wine. Bring to a boil, then reduce the heat to medium and let simmer for 2 to 3 minutes. Add salt to taste, then add bean sprouts and bring to a boil again. Cook for 1 minute more before reducing the heat to low again. Using a slotted spoon or fine-mesh strainer, scoop out vegetables and other solids and place in a heatproof serving bowl. Set aside.

3. In a small pot, heat ½ cup olive oil over medium-low heat. Stir in the smoked paprika. To test if the oil is ready for frying, dip a chopstick in and look for small bubbles to form around it. If this happens, your oil is ready.

4. While the oil is heating, turn up the heat under your broth to bring it back to a boil. Once boiling, reduce again to low and place the fish in the broth one piece at a time. Once all the fish is added, bring the soup to a boil for the last time, then immediately pour it on top of the vegetables in the serving bowl.

5. Sprinkle the dried chili peppers and peppercorns over the soup, then pour the heated oil directly on top to sizzle the chili peppers and peppercorns. Sprinkle with the remaining chopped green onion and top with a few slices of red bell pepper.

✦ ✦ ✦

SERVES: 2 | **PREP TIME:** 10 minutes + 30 minutes for marinating | **COOK TIME:** 20 minutes

pinch of salt + ½
teaspoon, divided

1 pound ground pork

1 egg, beaten

3 green onions, finely
chopped + 10 whole
green onions, for tying
the dumplings

1 tablespoon minced
fresh ginger

2 cloves garlic, minced

2 tablespoon soy sauce

1 tablespoon toasted
sesame oil + 1
teaspoon, divided

¼ teaspoon crushed
red pepper flakes

½ teaspoon black pepper

1 tablespoon paprika

10 large cabbage leaves,
root ends trimmed

2 cups pork bone broth

1 red chili pepper, sliced

SPECIAL EQUIPMENT
steamer basket

JADE DUMPLINGS

Switch out the dough for cabbage, and you've got the secret to making the most delicious Jade Dumplings. Cabbage gives this dish a gorgeous green color reminiscent of the jade gemstones it's named after. You might want to make this in bulk because you won't be able to stop after just one serving—and you never know when you may run across a hungry villager who will pay you for a bite of such delicious dumplings.

1. Fill a large saucepan a third full with water, add a pinch of salt, and bring to a boil over high heat.

2. While the water is coming to a boil, in a large mixing bowl, combine the ground pork, beaten egg, 3 chopped green onions, ginger, garlic, soy sauce, 1 tablespoon toasted sesame oil, crushed red pepper flakes, ½ teaspoon salt, pepper, and paprika. Mix to combine thoroughly, then set aside.

3. Place the cabbage leaves and 10 whole green onions in the boiling water for 3 minutes to soften them. Meanwhile, line a baking sheet with paper towels. Transfer the softened leaves and onions to the baking sheet and let cool.

4. Use the paper towels to pat off any excess water. Then spread out a cabbage leaf and place about 1½ tablespoons of the pork mixture in the middle of the leaf. Gather the leaf edges together and gently tie with a softened green onion. Repeat until all the cabbage leaves are filled with pork and tied shut.

5. In a pot that can hold a steamer basket, combine the 2 cups broth, the remaining 1 teaspoon sesame oil, and the chili slices. Set the steamer basket on top of the pot. (The pot should be filled to just below your basket so that the broth doesn't touch the dumplings.)

6. Place the dumplings in the steamer basket and bring the broth to a boil. Then cover with the pot lid and let steam until the pork is cooked through, about 15 minutes. To test, cut a dumpling open and make sure the pork has browned so no pink coloring remains.

7. Using tongs, carefully transfer the dumplings to a serving plate. Pour the chili broth you used for the steaming over the dumplings until they're sitting in a thin layer of the broth, then serve.

◆ ◆ ◆

SERVES: 2 | **PREP TIME:** 20 minutes | **COOK TIME:** 20 minutes

1 purple eggplant,
sliced in rounds

10 okra pods

10 peeled raw
shrimp, tails on

3 to 4 broccoli and/
or cauliflower florets

1 to 2 button
mushrooms, sliced

1 cup cherry blossom petals
(or fresh nettle leaves)

4 cups vegetable oil,
for deep-frying

1 cup all-purpose flour

¾ cup + 4 teaspoons
ice water

1 egg

1 teaspoon salt, or to taste

wasabi and/or soy
sauce, for serving

SPECIAL EQUIPMENT
deep fryer (optional)

CHERRY BLOSSOM TEMPURA

If you're lucky enough to live in a place with an abundance of cherry blossoms, this recipe is perfect for you. The next time you're admiring those delicate pink petals, collect a few and bring them back to your kitchen. The subtle floral flavor of cherry blossoms will serve to elevate this classic tempura dish. And yes, you can deep-fry cherry blossoms.

1. Pat all the vegetables and shrimp dry with a paper towel and set aside.

2. Add the oil to a deep fryer or a medium pot on the stovetop and heat to 320°F. (Use a thermometer to check the temperature, or dip the tip of a wooden or bamboo chopstick in the oil. If small bubbles appear around the chopstick, the oil is ready.)

3. While the oil is heating, prepare the tempura batter. Place the all-purpose flour in a large bowl. In a smaller bowl, whisk together the ice water and egg until fully combined. Scoop up and discard any surface foam.

4. Slowly pour the egg mixture into the flour while mixing with chopsticks or a wire whisk. Once all the egg mixture is in, continue whisking gently for about 15 seconds. Be careful not to overmix; it's okay to leave some lumps in your batter. It's important to keep the tempura batter cold, so set your bowl of batter inside a larger bowl filled with about 1 inch of ice water.

5. When the oil reaches the right temperature, start by dipping an eggplant slice in the cold batter, letting any excess batter drip off for a few seconds before very gently placing the eggplant in the hot oil. Repeat this with each individual ingredient you're going to deep fry, but make sure you don't overcrowd the deep fryer or cooking pot. The ingredients should take up only half of the surface area at any time. (Having too many ingredients in the pot at once will cause the oil temperature to drop.)

6. Deep-fry the vegetables and shrimp for 1 to 2 minutes each and the sakura petals or nettle leaves for 15 to 20 seconds, or until golden. Continue frying in batches until all the ingredients have been cooked, transferring each batch to a baking sheet or plate lined with paper towels to absorb excess oil. Between batches, skim any leftover tempura crumbs from the top of the oil so they don't burn and change the flavor of the oil.

7. Serve the tempura immediately with wasabi and/or soy sauce for dipping.

✦ ✦ ✦

SERVES: 2 | **PREP TIME:** 25 minutes | **COOK TIME:** 45 minutes

1 (8-ounce) package
soba noodles

2 tablespoons sesame oil

1 nori sheet, cut
into thin strips

pepper, to taste

soy sauce, for serving

COLD SOBA NOODLES

There's nothing like a cold bowl of soba noodles after a day spent collecting rhinoceros beetles, digging up treasure chests, or defeating samurai. The subtle buckwheat flavor of the noodles dunked in a cold soy sauce dip will refresh you in no time and get you ready to travel on to your next quest.

1. Over high heat, bring a medium pot of water to boil. Add the soba noodles and cook until they are chewy but still a little firm, about 4 to 5 minutes.

2. While the noodles are cooking, fill a large bowl with ice water.

3. Once the noodles are done cooking, strain them and place in the prepared ice water. Chill until the noodles are cold, about 3 minutes. Then strain again and toss with the sesame oil.

4. Place equal portions of noodles on serving plates and sprinkle with nori strips and a bit of pepper. Serve with soy sauce for dipping.

✦ ✦ ✦

SERVES: 2 | **PREP TIME:** 10 minutes | **COOK TIME:** 5 minutes

FOR THE FILLING:

1½ tablespoons
vegetable oil

1 green onion, sliced

¼ onion, diced

1 small carrot,
peeled and diced

3½ ounces Spam (or ¼ of
a 12-ounce can), cubed

2 to 3 button
mushrooms, diced

3 tablespoons frozen peas

1 cup cooked rice
(day-old is best)

1 tablespoon soy sauce

2 tablespoons ketchup

FOR THE OMELET:

1½ tablespoons
vegetable oil

3 large eggs

1 tablespoon milk

pinch of salt

ketchup, for serving

fresh parsley leaves,
for serving

OMURICE

Have you ever found yourself climbing a mountain, almost reaching the very top, when you suddenly begin to fall? Or you're just about to dodge an enemy attack, only to find yourself unable to sprint away and are instead sent flying backward from a damaging hit? We've all forgotten to keep our eyes on our stamina levels from time to time. But this delicious Omurice, or Japanese rice omelet, will help you save up stamina before your adventures even begin—making this recipe a must-have for any serious adventurer. The unforgettable taste of lightly cooked eggs wrapped around a flavorful pile of rice is a bonus.

1. To make the filling, in a large pan over medium heat, combine 1½ tablespoons oil with the sliced green onion and diced onion. Cook until fragrant, about 3 minutes. Add the diced carrot, Spam, mushrooms, and peas and cook for 3 to 4 more minutes, stirring occasionally.

2. Add the rice, soy sauce, and 2 tablespoons ketchup to the pan and mix well, making sure that everything is evenly coated. Transfer to a small bowl and press down to so the rice takes on the shape of the bowl.

3. To make the omelet, combine the eggs, milk, and salt in a bowl. Heat 1½ tablespoons oil in a medium nonstick skillet over medium heat and pour in the egg mixture. Lightly scramble for a few seconds, then cook the eggs until they are about 80 percent cooked through, then remove from the heat.

4. Place a large plate over the bowl of rice, holding it in the center, and flip carefully so the rice transfers to the plate in a dome shape.

5. Using a spatula, carefully slide the omelet out of the pan and over the rice. Drizzle with ketchup and top with parsley.

SERVES: 1 | **PREP TIME:** 5 minutes | **COOK TIME:** 10 minutes

Ingredients

12-ounce boneless pork loin, fat trimmed

⅓ cup shio koji seasoning

2½ teaspoons salt

1 cup water + 2 tablespoons, divided

½ head green cabbage, core removed and thinly sliced

zest and juice from 2 lemons

2 eggs

1 cup all-purpose flour

3 cups panko bread crumbs

5 to 6 cups vegetable oil, for frying

tonkatsu sauce

2 tablespoons Japanese Kewpie mayonnaise

8 slices Japanese milk bread or store-bought white bread, crusts removed

TIP: Shio koji is a simple mixture of rice koji, water, and salt that adds a ton of flavor to marinades for seafood, poultry, veggies, and more. It can be found at most Japanese grocery stores or in the Asian food section at your local supermarket. You can also easily buy shio koji online.

PORK CUTLET SANDWICH

Throughout your travels, you've probably come across a few fried pork cutlet recipes—pork served over rice, eggs, noodles, curry, and more. And while all are delicious, sometimes you need something a little more manageable for the road. A Pork Cutlet Sandwich, with its fluffy bread surrounding the crispiest pork cutlet, is the perfect lunch to munch on as you traverse snowy mountains or arid deserts.

1. To prepare the pork cutlets, slice the pork loin into 4 equal pieces. Place each slice in a sealed plastic bag with all the air removed or between 2 sheets of plastic wrap. Using a meat tenderizer, gently pound each slice until it is about 6 inches wide and ¼ inch thick.

2. In a medium bowl, combine the shio koji, 2 teaspoons salt, and 1 cup water; stir well until the salt is fully dissolved. Add the pork pieces, then cover and chill in the refrigerator for 8 hours or overnight.

3. Just before the pork is done chilling, place the cabbage in a medium bowl. Zest both lemons over the cabbage and then add the juice from the lemons. Season with ½ teaspoon salt and toss with your hands until the cabbage is fully coated and slightly wilted. Cover and chill until ready to use.

4. After the pork has chilled, remove it from the refrigerator, drain, and set aside. Line a rimmed baking sheet with paper towels, set a wire rack on top, and place near the stovetop.

5. In a shallow dish, whisk together the eggs and 2 tablespoons water. Place the flour and the bread crumbs in 2 more shallow dishes. Working with a single pork cutlet at a time, first coat it in the flour, shaking off any excess. Then dip it in the eggs and finally in the bread crumbs, pressing firmly into the crumbs on both sides to make sure they stick. Transfer to another rimmed baking sheet or a platter.

6. Pour oil into a medium-deep pot so that it comes about 2 inches up the side. Heat over medium-high heat until an instant-read thermometer reads between 350°F and 365°F. Using chopsticks or tongs, lower a cutlet vertically into the pan, letting it slide away into the oil until it lies flat. Use the chopsticks or tongs to keep the pork fully submerged in the oil until the underside is golden brown, about 1 minute. Gently flip and cook the other side until it is also golden brown, about 1 more minute. Then transfer the cutlet to the prepared wire rack over the paper towel–lined baking sheet. Repeat with the remaining pork cutlets.

7. Drizzle tonkatsu sauce over the cutlets and let rest for a few minutes. Then spread Kewpie mayonnaise on half of the bread slices and add a few cabbage leaves. Top with a pork cutlet and a second slice of bread, then cut each sandwich in half.

◆ ◆ ◆

SERVES: 4 | **PREP TIME:** 15 minutes + 8 hours chilling time | **COOK TIME:** 10 minutes

4 boneless, skinless chicken thighs

1½ cups buttermilk

1 tablespoon hot sauce

2 teaspoons paprika, divided

2 teaspoons salt, divided

2 teaspoons onion powder, divided

2 teaspoons garlic powder, divided

1 teaspoon pepper, divided

1¾ cups all-purpose flour

1 teaspoon baking powder

1 teaspoon dried oregano

4 to 5 cups vegetable oil, for deep frying

½ cup mayonnaise

1 tablespoon honey

3 cloves garlic, minced

1 tablespoon lemon juice

4 burger buns

8 lettuce leaves

CRISPY CHICKEN SANDWICH

Part of being a successful adventurer is simply being in the right place at the right time. If you were lucky enough to obtain this recipe during a special culinary event, then you know how healing a Crispy Chicken Sandwich can be. This is definitely a sandwich you'll keep wanting to come back to—for both the HP boost and the flavor!

1. Place each chicken thigh in a sealed plastic bag with the air removed, or between sheets of plastic wrap. Using a meat tenderizer, gently pound until each thigh is about ½ inch thick.

2. To make the marinade, add the buttermilk, hot sauce, 1 teaspoon paprika, 1 teaspoon salt, 1 teaspoon onion powder, 1 teaspoon garlic powder, and ½ teaspoon pepper to a large bowl. Mix well until thoroughly combined. Add the chicken thighs and toss, making sure each thigh is evenly coated. Cover the bowl with plastic wrap and refrigerate for 5 hours, or overnight. Remove from the fridge at least 30 minutes before you bread the chicken.

3. In a medium bowl, combine the flour, 1 teaspoon paprika, baking powder, oregano, 1 teaspoon salt, 1 teaspoon onion powder, 1 teaspoon garlic powder, and ½ teaspoon pepper. Dredge the thighs one by one in the mixture, pressing each thigh into the breading to make sure it is completely coated before shaking off any excess. Set aside.

4. Pour 3 to 4 cups of oil into a deep pan or large pot; the oil should come about 1 inch up the side. Heat to 350°F over medium-high heat. While it is heating, line a baking sheet with parchment paper, place a wire rack on top, and set aside.

5. Fry the chicken thighs individually, gently placing them in the hot oil and frying for 3 to 4 minutes on each side, until golden brown. They should reach an internal temperature of 165°F (you can check with an instant-read thermometer).

6. Carefully remove the chicken from the oil, using tongs or a slotted spoon, and transfer to the wire rack. If the oil temp has dropped during frying, bring it back up to 350°F before frying the next piece. Repeat until all the thighs are cooked.

7. To make the honey garlic mayo, in a small bowl whisk together the mayonnaise, honey, minced garlic, and lemon juice.

8. To assemble the sandwiches, start by lightly toasting the buns in the oven or toaster. Spread honey garlic mayo onto a toasted bottom bun, then add a fried chicken thigh and 1 or 2 lettuce leaves. Spread the top half of the bun with more honey garlic mayo and place over the chicken. Repeat to make all 4 sandwiches.

◆ ◆ ◆

SERVES: 4 | **PREP TIME:** 20 minutes | **COOK TIME:** 30 to 35 minutes

FOR THE MARINATED CHICKEN:

2 pounds boneless, skinless chicken thigh

1 garlic clove, minced

1 tablespoon ground coriander

1 tablespoon ground turmeric

1 tablespoon ground cumin

1 teaspoon ground cayenne pepper, or to taste

2 teaspoons smoked paprika

salt and pepper, to taste

juice from 1 lemon

3 tablespoons olive oil + more, for frying

FOR THE YOGURT SAUCE:

1 cup plain Greek yogurt

1 clove garlic, minced

1 teaspoon ground cumin

1 tablespoon lemon juice

salt and pepper, to taste

FOR THE WRAP:

4 flatbreads

sliced lettuce leaves

2 to 3 tomatoes, sliced

½ red onion, finely sliced

CHICKEN SHAWARMA

When passing through various ports, cities, and towns, Travelers find all kinds of sweet and savory street food, from Fried Radish on a Stick (page 12) and Colorful Dango (page 125) to this tasty Chicken Shawarma. Occasionally it's nice to buy your food at a local food stall rather than cook it yourself, but once you've tasted this wrap—filled with the juiciest roasted chicken and fresh vegetables—you'll definitely want to have the recipe on hand!

1. Combine chicken and marinade ingredients in a large plastic bag. Seal and massage from the outside to thoroughly coat the chicken. Place in the refrigerator to marinate overnight.

2. Combine the yogurt sauce ingredients in a small bowl and mix well. Cover and refrigerate.

3. Once the chicken is marinated, heat a large nonstick skillet over medium-high heat and add about 1 tablespoon oil.

4. Place the chicken pieces in the skillet and cook for 5 minutes, until underside starts to crisp up and char. Flip and brown the other side for 3 to 4 minutes.

5. Transfer the cooked chicken to a plate and cover to keep warm. Set aside to rest for 5 minutes, then cut into slices.

6. To arrange the wraps, spread yogurt sauce over each flatbread and then add lettuce, sliced tomato, red onion, and chicken. Roll up and dig in!

◆ ◆ ◆

SERVES: 4 | **PREP TIME:** 10 minutes + overnight marinating | **COOK TIME:** 10 minutes

THE UNOFFICIAL GENSHIN IMPACT COOKBOOK

Simple Onigiri

3 cups cooked sushi
rice, cooled

5 tablespoons
furikake seasoning

water

salt

1 (4.5-ounce) can tuna
in olive oil, drained

1½ tablespoons Japanese
Kewpie mayonnaise

1 teaspoon sriracha
hot sauce

½ teaspoon rice vinegar

1 green onion (green
parts only), finely sliced

3 nori sheets, cut into
thin rectangles

wasabi, for serving

soy sauce, for serving

Take lunch to go as you hurry on to your next quest! The crunchy sheets of nori wrapped around the base of these rice balls makes it easy to grab one and start munching as you walk, run, or even climb to your destination.

1. Place the sushi rice in a large mixing bowl. Add the furikake and mix evenly.

2. Divide the rice into equal portions, approximately 1 large handful for each onigiri.

3. To make the filling, in a medium bowl mix the tuna, mayonnaise, sriracha, and rice vinegar with a fork until evenly combined. Stir in the green onions and set aside.

4. Wet your hands with water and rub together with a pinch or two of salt. This keeps the rice from sticking to your hands and helps it stay fresh longer.

5. Pick up 1 portion of rice and shape it into a ball. Using your fingertips, make a small well in the rice ball and add about 1 teaspoon of tuna filling. Close the well by covering it with rice, then gently press and squeeze the rice ball into a triangular shape, rotating it so that it's even on all sides.

6. Place a nori rectangle under the onigiri and fold the edges up toward the middle. Repeat with the remaining rice portions.

7. Serve on a serving plate garnished with wasabi and a side of soy sauce.

SERVES: 4 | **PREP TIME:** 20 minutes

5 ounces raw salmon,
thinly sliced

5 ounces raw tuna,
thinly sliced

5 ounces raw octopus,
thinly sliced

5 large raw shrimp,
shelled, tail on

wasabi, for serving

soy sauce, for serving

ginger paste, for serving

edible flowers, for
decoration

SASHIMI SELECTION

Grab your fishing pole and head out to the nearest fishing spot because you'll to want to use the freshest ingredients possible for this dish. Besides fresh fish, the key to an impeccable plate of sashimi is excellent knifework skill. Cutting the delicate fish at just the right angle and to the perfect size will elevate this platter to a work of art. Looks like all those hours spent wielding a sword are about to pay off!

1. Place the sliced salmon, tuna, octopus, and shrimp on a serving plate. Decorate the plate with flowers for a festive touch.

2. Serve with wasabi, soy sauce, and/or ginger paste.

SERVES: 2 | **PREP TIME:** 10 minutes

FOR THE SALAD:

2 cups diced butternut squash

1 tablespoon olive oil

salt and pepper, to taste

4 large eggs

2 boneless, skinless chicken breasts (optional)

½ cup chopped raw bacon (optional)

4 heads Little Gem lettuce

1 Golden Delicious (or other yellow) apple, cored and thinly sliced

2 avocados, sliced

½ cup dried figs, sliced

½ cup crumbled goat cheese

½ cup cubed white cheddar cheese

⅓ cup toasted sunflower seeds

FOR THE DRESSING:

3 tablespoons olive oil

3 tablespoons mayonnaise

juice from 1 lemon

1 tablespoon maple syrup

1 teaspoon Dijon mustard

2 cloves garlic, minced

salt and pepper, to taste

SPECIAL EQUIPMENT

air fryer (optional)

STRENGTHENING SALAD

This refreshing vegetarian salad will satisfy adventurers looking to create a delicious meal from all the fruits and veggies collected as they travel from one town to the next. But if you're looking for some extra protein to get you through a particularly grueling quest, feel free to use your hunting skills to top this salad with some savory meat.

1. Preheat the oven to 400°F and line a baking sheet with parchment paper. Spread the squash cubes in a single layer on the baking sheet, then drizzle with 1 tablespoon olive oil and sprinkle with salt and pepper. Toss to coat.

2. Bake until tender, about 15 to 20 minutes.

3. While the squash is cooking, place the eggs in a medium pot. Pour in enough cool water so they are fully submerged. Bring the water to a boil over high heat, then lower the heat and simmer the eggs to the desired doneness—4 minutes for soft-boiled, 6 minutes for medium-boiled, or 10 minutes for hard-boiled. (I personally like medium-boiled the best.)

4. Fill a medium bowl with ice water and use a slotted spoon to transfer the cooked eggs into the ice water to cool for about 5 minutes. Then peel the eggs, cut them into quarters, and set aside.

5. If making the protein-packed version of this salad, cook the chicken breasts on a lined baking sheet in the oven at 450°F for 15 to 18 minutes or in the air fryer at 400°F for 12 to 16 minutes. Flip halfway through whether you're using the oven or air fryer.

6. Continuing with the protein, while the chicken is cooking, fry the chopped bacon in a small skillet over medium heat for 4 minutes or until crispy, then transfer to a paper towel–lined plate and pat to remove excess grease. Set aside.

7. When the chicken is ready, remove it from the oven or air fryer and let rest for 5 minutes, then cut into cubes.

8. To make the dressing, in a small bowl whisk together all the dressing ingredients.

9. To arrange the salad, place the Little Gem leaves in a large salad bowl. Top with the butternut squash, egg quarters, and apple slices. If using, add the chicken and bacon.

10. Drizzle on the dressing, then scatter the avocado and figs slices, goat cheese, cheddar cheese, and sunflower seeds over the top. Sprinkle with extra pepper and serve.

◆ ◆ ◆

SERVES: 2 | **PREP TIME:** 15 minutes |
COOK TIME: 20 to 40 minutes

DINNER

3 teaspoons salt + more, to taste, divided

2 teaspoons pepper + more, to taste, divided

1 whole chicken

2½ lemons, divided

2 tablespoons olive oil

2 sprigs fresh rosemary

4 to 5 sprigs fresh thyme

3 sprigs fresh oregano

¼ cup honey

SPECIAL EQUIPMENT
shallow roasting pan

Sweet Roasted Chicken

Despite what many locals may think, this dish really is made of chicken, not pigeons! This is a classic dish that every Traveler learns when they first start their journey. The honey here pairs beautifully with an assortment of herbs to elevate simple chicken into a decadent dish enjoyed by all (unless you're a certain princess with a talking crow).

1. In a small bowl, combine the 3 teaspoons salt and 2 teaspoons pepper, then rub the mixture all over the outside of the chicken.

2. Place the chicken in a resealable plastic bag and pour in any remaining salt and pepper mix. Juice 2 lemons and add the juice to the bag. Seal the bag and gently massage to coat the chicken in the lemon juice.

3. Place the bagged chicken on a large plate and let it chill in the refrigerator for at least 6 hours, or overnight. Flip the bag occasionally so that the entire chicken stays coated with lemon juice.

4. When the chicken is finished marinating, place an oven rack in the bottom third of the oven and preheat the oven to 400°F.

5. Discard the marinade and pat the chicken dry with paper towels, then brush all over with olive oil. Sprinkle with more salt and pepper, making sure to sprinkle some in the cavity. Cut half a lemon into wedges, then place the wedges and the fresh herbs in the cavity.

6. Set the chicken on a wire rack in a shallow roasting pan or on a rimmed baking sheet. Roast uncovered for 20 minutes, then reduce oven temperature to 350°F and roast for another 45 minutes.

7. While the chicken is roasting, put the honey in a microwave-safe bowl and heat in the microwave for about 3 minutes, or until melted. Alternatively, melt the honey in a saucepan over medium heat for about 5 minutes, stirring occasionally.

8. Once the chicken is done cooking, remove from the oven and generously coat the top and sides of the chicken with the warmed honey. Return to the oven and roast for another 10 to 15 minutes, or until an instant-read thermometer shows an internal temperature of 160°F for the breast portion and 170°F for the thigh. (You can also tell that the chicken is thoroughly cooked if it releases clear juices when you cut into it.) Check during last few minutes of cooking to make sure the honey doesn't burn. If the skin is becoming too dark and the chicken still isn't done, loosely cover with aluminum foil. About 5 minutes before the chicken is done roasting, brush with honey again.

9. Remove the chicken from the oven, transfer it to a serving platter, and tent with aluminum foil. Let rest for 15 minutes and then serve.

SERVES: 4 | **PREP TIME:** 15 minutes + 6 hours for marinating | **COOK TIME:** 2½ hours

3 tablespoons olive oil

½ onion, chopped

2 cloves garlic, minced

1½ teaspoons
smoked paprika

1 teaspoon ground cumin

1 pound ground beef

salt and pepper, to taste

1 tablespoon tomato paste

½ cup tomato sauce

2 thick pita breads,
cut in half

4 tablespoons mayonnaise

4 to 6 lettuce leaves

1 globe tomato (such as
beefsteak), cut into slices

STUFFED PITA

This delicious flatbread is stuffed with spiced meat and fresh, crunchy veggies, then topped with a light sauce that marries the ingredients together. The harmony of flavors will remind you of loyal friendship, and in particular your newfound friendship with a certain forest ranger trainee.

1. In a frying pan over medium heat, heat the oil and cook the onion until translucent, about 5 minutes. Add the garlic, smoked paprika, and cumin and cook for 30 seconds while stirring.

2. Add the ground beef, breaking it up with a large spoon or a spatula. Cook until browned, about 5 minutes, stirring frequently. Add the salt, pepper, tomato paste, and tomato sauce and cook, stirring occasionally, until the liquid is almost fully reduced.

3. Heat the pita bread halves in a dry frying pan over medium-high heat for about 2 to 3 minutes. Flip halfway through.

4. Spread mayonnaise inside each bread pocket and add lettuce leaves and tomato slices. Stuff with the ground beef mixture to serve.

SERVES: 2 | **PREP TIME:** 10 minutes | **COOK TIME:** 20 minutes

BUTTERY GRILLED FISH

4 (8-ounce) cod cutlets

salt and pepper, to taste

2 tablespoons all-purpose flour

2 tablespoons vegetable oil

2 tablespoons unsalted butter

2 cloves garlic, minced

½ teaspoon dried mint

2 teaspoons lemon juice

½ teaspoon lemon zest

fresh chopped mint, for serving

fresh chopped parsley, for serving

When cooked to perfection, this fish should melt in your mouth. That may have something to do with all the butter you gently fry in! While this dish may appear delicate, you'll find that it will give you the energy you need to bolster your defenses against even the most skilled adversaries.

1. Using paper towels, pat the fish cutlets dry. Season with salt and pepper.

2. Place the flour in a shallow bowl. Lightly coat both sides of the fish cutlets in the flour. Shake off any excess.

3. In a large frying pan over medium-high heat, bring the oil to a simmer. Add the fish cutlets and cook for 4 to 6 minutes, then turn over. (Wait until the fish lifts easily off the skillet before turning it.) Cook for 4 minutes more, or until the fish flakes easily with a fork. Transfer the cod to a serving plate and tent with foil to keep warm. Wipe out the skillet with a paper towel.

4. Melt the butter in the skillet over medium-high heat. Add the garlic and cook for 1 minute, or until fragrant, stirring frequently.

5. Remove the skillet from the heat and stir in the dried mint. The lemon juice, and lemon zest. Drizzle the butter sauce over each cod cutlet. Sprinkle with the fresh herbs to serve.

✦ ✦ ✦

SERVES: 4 | **PREP TIME:** 10 minutes | **COOK TIME:** 9 to 11 minutes

FIRED-UP BOLOGNESE

6 tablespoons unsalted butter, cut into 1 tablespoon pieces

1 medium onion, finely chopped

2 large carrots, peeled and finely chopped

3 stalks celery, finely chopped

4 cloves garlic, minced

2 pounds 85% lean ground beef

salt and pepper, to taste

1½ cups whole milk

2 (28-ounce) cans cubed tomatoes in puree

1 cup dry white wine

⅓ cup fresh basil leaves, chopped

1 tablespoon dried oregano

1 parmesan cheese rind

unsalted chicken stock or broth, as needed to thin sauce

1 cup grated parmesan cheese, for serving

1 (1-pound) package spaghetti

A pasta dish with a hearty meat and tomato sauce is infinitely comforting, making Fired-Up Bolognese one of the best recovery dishes out there. Next time you've finished a particularly grueling quest or battled your way through the latest domain, you won't have to drag yourself to the nearest restaurant or food stand to find a fortifying meal. You can make this dish from the comfort of your own campfire.

1. Melt 1½ tablespoons of the butter in a large pot over medium-high heat. Add the onion, carrots, and celery and sauté for 4 minutes, stirring occasionally. Add the garlic and sauté for 1 minute longer. Transfer the mixture to a large plate.

2. Melt another 1½ tablespoons butter in the same pot over medium-high heat. Add the beef and break it up, using a large spoon. Season lightly with salt and pepper. Cook until browned, about 5 minutes, stirring frequently.

3. Transfer the vegetables back to the pot with the beef, pour in the milk, and stir. Bring to a simmer and then reduce the heat to medium-low. Let simmer until most of the milk has evaporated and just the fat remains, about 20 minutes.

4. Stir in the tomatoes, wine, basil, oregano, and parmesan rind. Bring the mixture to a simmer, then reduce the heat to very low. Let simmer for 4 hours, stirring occasionally and thinning with broth if the sauce is becoming too thick.

5. Season lightly with salt and pepper to taste as it cooks. Keep in mind that the saltiness will become more concentrated as the sauce is reduced, so be careful not to overdo it. You can always add more later.

6. Remove the parmesan rind and add the remaining 3 tablespoons butter, stirring until melted. Remove from heat.

7. Cook the spaghetti according to the package instructions, then drain well and gently toss with the sauce, or spoon the sauce over the pasta to serve.

◆ ◆ ◆

SERVES: 4 | **PREP TIME:** 20 minutes | **COOK TIME:** 4½ hours

Ingredients

3 ounces pork fat (preferably leaf lard or fatback)

2 cups pork bone broth

2 cups unsweetened soy milk

2 cups dashi stock

1 cup fresh bean sprouts

1 packet instant ramen noodles

2 to 3 slices chashu pork

3 to 4 tablespoons tsuyu (Japanese soup base) or chashu tare

1 green onion, chopped, for serving

1 ramen egg or soft-boiled egg, halved

1 clove garlic (optional)

TIP: Several kinds of pork fat can be found in your local grocery store or—more easily—online. Leaf lard and fatback are two of the higher-quality versions and therefore are best for this recipe. Lard and leaf lard aren't the same thing, so don't get them mixed up! Another common type of pork fat is caul, but it can be difficult to clean and prepare for cooking, so I'd avoid using it if you can!

PORK BROTH RAMEN

The secret to ramen is the broth—simmering pork fat, broth, and dashi together to create a deeply flavorful broth that will absorb into your springy noodles and make a dish that you'll want to eat over and over again. And if you're feeling more on the adventurous side, try experimenting with all kinds of toppings, from soft-boiled eggs and pork slices to beansprouts, green onions, and garlic!

1. Place the pork fat in a medium pot and add water until the fat is completely covered. Bring to a boil over medium-high heat and cook for 5 to 7 minutes, or until fork tender.

2. Remove the pork fat from the pot, discard the water, and cut the fat into small chunks. Place in a blender, add the pork bone broth, and blend on high speed until smooth, about 1 to 2 minutes. Pour the mixture back into the pot, then add the unsweetened soy milk and dashi stock. Stir well and bring to a simmer over low heat, stirring occasionally.

3. In another medium pot, bring water to a boil to blanch the bean sprouts for 1 minute, then scoop them out with a slotted spoon and set aside. In the same boiling water, cook the instant ramen noodles according to the packet instructions, leaving out any seasoning that came with the noodles.

4. While the noodles are cooking, prepare the chashu pork by searing it in a dry pan over high heat, by torching it, or by broiling it at a high temperature for 3 to 5 minutes. Set aside.

5. Add the tsuyu or chashu tare to a serving bowl, carefully pour in 1½ cups of the prepared broth, and mix well. Drain the cooked noodles and add them to the serving bowl.

6. Arrange toppings of blanched bean sprouts, chopped green onions, chashu pork slices, and halved ramen egg over the noodles. Grate a clove of garlic on top to serve, if desired.

SERVES: 1 | **PREP TIME:** 10 minutes | **COOK TIME:** 15 minutes

FOR THE SMOKED CHICKEN:

1 tablespoon paprika

½ tablespoon smoked paprika

1 tablespoon garlic powder

1 teaspoon salt

½ tablespoon onion powder

1 teaspoon pepper

⅓ cup brown sugar, packed

4 boneless, skinless chicken breasts

2 tablespoons Dijon mustard

cabbage leaves, for serving

sliced red onion, for serving

FOR THE POTATOES:

1 large russet potato, peeled and cut into ½-inch cubes

2 tablespoons olive oil

salt and pepper, to taste

1 teaspoon dried parsley

SPECIAL EQUIPMENT

Smoker or wood chips

While scaling one of the tallest towers of a certain northern dragon's lair, adventurers may find a treasure chest along the way. But it doesn't contain gold coins, precious ore, or historical artifacts. Instead, you'll find a recipe for this delicious smoked chicken—a delicacy of the north. After climbing all that way, your stamina is likely depleted, so you'll want to whip up a campfire, gather supplies, and cook this dish as soon as possible.

1. If using an electric smoker, preheat it to 225°F and place a pan of water on the lower rack. If using an oven, first soak a quart of wood chips in water for an hour. Then drain the wood chips, reserving ¼ cup of the water. Move an oven rack to the oven floor and set the oven temperature to 225°F. Pour both the water-soaked chips and the ¼ cup reserved soaking water into the bottom of a roasting pan and place on the rack on the oven floor.

2. In a medium bowl, combine the seasonings and brown sugar for the Smoked Chicken; mix well.

3. While the smoker or oven is heating, rub each chicken breast with Dijon mustard and coat both sides generously with the seasoning mix.

4. Insert an instant-read thermometer into the center of the thickest chicken breast, through the side, to track the internal temperature.

5. Place the chicken breasts on the smoker when it's ready and close the lid immediately. Smoke until the chicken reaches a temperature of 160°F. If using an oven, insert a rack in the middle of the oven. Seal the roasting pan with foil and set it on top of the rack. Make sure that the foil is tented so there is room for smoke to circulate. The chicken breasts are ready when the thermometer reaches 160°F, about 1 hour.

6. While the chicken is cooking, rinse the cubed potatoes and transfer to a large pot. Cover with water and bring to a boil over high heat. Then lower the heat and simmer for about 10 minutes, until the potatoes are slightly tender when you test them with a knife but not completely cooked through. Drain well.

7. In a large frying pan over medium-high heat, heat the oil until it's smoking. Add the potatoes and season with salt, pepper, and dried parsley. Toss every few minutes until the potatoes are fork tender, about 15 to 20 minutes.

8. When the chicken reaches an internal temperature of 160°F, remove it from the smoker or oven, loosely tent it with aluminum foil, and let it rest for 5 to 10 minutes.

9. Garnish a serving plate with cabbage leaves. Slice the chicken and serve on top of cabbage leaves alongside sautéed potatoes and red onion.

◆ ◆ ◆

SERVES: 4 | **PREP TIME:** 15 minutes | **COOK TIME:** 1½ hours

FOR THE CRUST:

1½ cups warm water (between 100°F and 110°F)

2¼ teaspoons instant yeast

1 tablespoon honey

1¼ cups white whole-wheat flour

2 tablespoons olive oil + more, for oiling bowl

1½ teaspoon salt

2½ cups all-purpose flour + more, as needed

¼ cup yellow cornmeal

FOR THE TOPPING:

11 ounces fresh mozzarella cheese, sliced

1 cup ricotta cheese

½ teaspoon dried thyme

½ teaspoon dried oregano

1 pound cremini mushrooms, thinly sliced

1 green bell pepper, chopped

salt and pepper, to taste

fresh basil leaves, for serving

SPECIAL EQUIPMENT

stand mixer with dough hook or paddle attachment

WHITE MUSHROOM PIZZA

You may come across endless types of pizza during your travels. But nothing else tastes quite like this White Mushroom Pizza, with its heaping toppings of cheese, mushrooms, and fresh herbs. Get ready for a dish that your travel companions will want you to make again and again.

1. To make the dough for the pizza crust, gently whisk the warm water, yeast, and honey in the bowl of a stand mixer fitted with dough hook or paddle attachment. Let stand until the mixture turns foamy, about 5 minutes.

2. Add the white whole-wheat flour, olive oil, and salt and mix at medium-low speed until well combined, about 2 minutes. Add the all-purpose flour ½ cup at a time while mixer is still beating, until a smooth ball of dough is formed. When touched, the dough should feel slightly tacky and bouncy. Increase the mixer speed to medium-high and beat for another 5 minutes.

3. Place the dough in a large, lightly oiled bowl and turn it around a few times to coat all over with the oil. Cover with a clean dish towel or plastic wrap and let rise at room temperature for 45 minutes, or until the dough has doubled in size.

4. Preheat the oven to 450°F. Line a baking sheet with parchment paper and set aside.

5. Once risen, lightly flour your work surface remove the dough from the bowl, and knead for 3 minutes. Wipe the excess flour off your work surface, then sprinkle with cornmeal. Place the dough on top of cornmeal and use a rolling pin to roll the dough into a 12-inch round, then transfer it to the prepared baking sheet.

6. Top with the mozzarella slices and dollops of ricotta. Sprinkle with dried thyme and oregano and arrange sliced mushrooms and green peppers over the top. Sprinkle on salt and pepper to taste.

7. Place the pizza on the middle rack of the oven and bake for 15 to 20 minutes, or until the crust is golden brown and the cheese has melted. Decorate with fresh basil leaves and serve immediately.

◆ ◆ ◆

SERVES: 2 | **PREP TIME:** 20 minutes + 45 minutes for dough-rising | **COOK TIME:** 20 minutes

3 pounds boneless beef chuck roast, cut into 1-inch cubes

2 teaspoons salt + more, to taste, divided

1 teaspoon pepper + more, to taste, divided

2 tablespoons vegetable oil

5 cups beef stock

3 large carrots, peeled and chopped

2 cups fresh okra pods

2 onions, diced

2 stalks celery, diced

1 red bell pepper, diced

1 yellow bell pepper, diced

¼ cup paprika

4 cloves garlic, minced

1 (8-ounce) can tomato sauce

1 Roma tomato, diced

1 tablespoon soy sauce

2 bay leaves

3 sprigs fresh thyme

3 large russet potatoes, peeled and cubed

2 tablespoons all-purpose flour

¼ cup water

1½ tablespoons apple cider vinegar

fresh parsley or fresh cilantro, chopped, for serving

WARMING GOULASH

Of all the dishes a Traveler needs on the road, this Warming Goulash might just be the most important. Not only does the medley of hearty vegetables, meat, and spices create a phenomenally flavorful dish, but this hot stew is known for keeping harsh cold temperatures at bay. If you ever find yourself stranded on an icy road or snowy mountain, whip up this dish to keep yourself warm.

1. Move an oven rack to the lower third of the oven. Preheat the oven to 300°F.

2. In a large bowl, season the beef chunks generously with the 2 teaspoons salt and 1 teaspoon pepper and set aside. Add the oil to a Dutch oven or oven-safe stockpot and heat on the stovetop over medium-high heat. Add the seasoned meat and cook until the beef cubes are browning around the edges, about 10 minutes. Transfer the beef back to the bowl and set aside.

3. Reduce the heat to medium-low. Add the sliced carrots and okra to the Dutch oven or stockpot and season to taste with salt and pepper. Cook for about 4 minutes, then transfer to a bowl and set aside. Add the onion, celery, and bell peppers to the pot and cook, stirring occasionally, until the onion and peppers are soft and starting to brown, about 8 minutes.

4. Add the paprika and minced garlic and cook about 1 more minute, until the garlic is fragrant. Pour in the stock, tomato sauce, diced tomatoes, and soy sauce. Sprinkle on the bay leaves and thyme and stir to combine.

5. Add the beef chunks back into the cooking pot and turn the heat up to medium. Stirring well, bring everything to a simmer.

6. Once the mixture is simmering, transfer the pot to the oven, cover it with a lid set slightly off the top, and cook for 1 hour. Adjust the oven temperature if necessary to maintain a low simmer.

THE UNOFFICIAL GENSHIN IMPACT COOKBOOK

7. Remove the goulash from the oven and add the potatoes and the reserved carrots and okra. Return to the oven with the lid partially covering the pot again. Cook until the broth has thickened and the beef and potatoes are fork tender, about 45 minutes. Remove the lid. Using a ladle, skim any excess fat from the surface and discard.

8. In a small bowl, mix together the 2 tablespoons flour and ¼ cup water. Pour over the goulash and stir gently until well combined. Cook in the oven for another 5 minutes.

9. Remove from the oven, stir in the vinegar, and season to taste with salt and pepper, if necessary.

10. Serve in individual bowls and top with fresh parsley or cilantro.

✦ ✦ ✦

SERVES: 6 | **PREP TIME:** 20 minutes | **COOK TIME:** 2¼ hours

¾ cup soy sauce +
⅛ cup, divided

¼ cup light brown
sugar, packed

2½ tablespoons
minced garlic

1 teaspoon onion powder

1 teaspoon paprika

½ teaspoon dried oregano

2 scallions, chopped

2 pounds boneless,
skin-on pork shoulder

5 medium Yukon Gold
potatoes, chopped
into ½-inch chunks

2 carrots, peeled and sliced

10 cloves garlic

2 tablespoon olive oil

salt and pepper, to taste

1 cup dark brown
sugar, packed

½ cup honey

HONEY-GLAZED ROAST

If you're trying to impress a certain bow-wielding outrider, offering this home-cooked Honey-Glazed Roast might just be the way to do it. It's known to be her favorite dish, and it will fast become one of your favorites, too. You can't go wrong with succulent pork roast covered with a sweet-and-savory glaze and accompanied by perfectly seasoned veggies—a superb meal.

1. In a large bowl, combine the ¾ cup soy sauce with the light brown sugar, minced garlic, onion powder, paprika, oregano, and chopped scallions.

2. Using a sharp knife, score the fat layer of the pork in diamond shapes.

3. Place the pork in the soy sauce marinade and turn to coat evenly. Cover with plastic wrap and place in the fridge to marinate for 1 hour.

4. Preheat the oven to 275°F. Place the potatoes, carrots, and garlic cloves on a rimmed baking sheet and toss with the 2 tablespoons oil, salt, and pepper. Place the marinated pork on top of the veggies in the middle of the baking sheet. Bake for 1 hour, then remove from the oven.

5. Increase the oven temperature to 500°F. In a small bowl, combine the dark brown sugar, honey, and remaining ⅛ cup soy sauce, stirring until smooth.

6. Spoon the honey glaze over the top of the pork. Return to the oven and bake for 15 to 20 minutes, until the sugar is caramelized and the top of the pork is crispy.

7. Transfer the pork and vegetables to a serving plate. Spoon the reserved pan juices on top of the pork to serve.

SERVES: 4 | **PREP TIME:** 10 minutes + 1 hour for marinating | **COOK TIME:** 1 hour 20 minutes

1 teaspoon salt

½ teaspoon pepper

1 teaspoon dried thyme

1 teaspoon garlic powder

2 (1-pound) boneless strip steaks, 1½ inches thick

1 tablespoon olive oil

GRILLED STEAK

Sometimes the best way to rest up and recover from a day's adventuring is to make a simple, juicy steak. Grilled Steak is a dish any beginner can master, and it's perfect for Travelers who are just starting out on their epic quest. One small bite and you'll feel like all your hard work has been worth it!

1. Combine the dried seasonings in a small bowl. Rub both sides of each steak with olive oil, then generously season all over with your seasoning mixture.

2. Light two of the grill burners and heat on high for 10 minutes, or until the temperature reaches 500°F. Add the steaks to the lit burners, close the grill lid, and sear for 1 to 2 minutes. Then flip the steaks, close the grill lid again, and sear for 1 more minute.

3. Open the grill lid and move the steaks to the unlit portion of the grill. Continue cooking for 7 more minutes, grill lid closed, until the steaks reach medium-rare doneness.

4. Transfer the steaks to a large plate and let rest for at least 5 minutes. Sprinkle with salt and black pepper, if desired, and serve.

SERVES: 2 | PREP TIME: 15 minutes | COOK TIME: 10 minutes + 5 minutes resting

FOR THE STIR-FRY:

1 pound large raw shrimp

5 cups water

4 tablespoons (½ stick) unsalted butter, divided

salt and pepper, to taste

1 cup peas (fresh or frozen)

1 clove garlic, minced

FOR THE SAUCE:

½ cup (1 stick) unsalted butter

¾ cup corn starch

4½ cups broth from cooking the shrimp

salt and pepper, to taste

SIMPLE SHRIMP STIR FRY

Unlike any stir-fry you may have tried before, this dish keeps it simple and makes the shrimp the star of the plate. Some regions consider stir-fried shrimp a delicacy worthy of feasts and banquets, while others pull out this recipe when a comforting home-cooked meal is needed.

1. Place the shrimp in a medium pot over high heat and cover with 5 cups water. Bring to a boil, then lower the heat and simmer for 5 minutes. Remove from the heat and drain well, reserving 4½ cups of the liquid.

2. Once cooled, peel the shrimp. Heat a large wok or frying pan over medium heat and add 2 tablespoons of butter. Add the shrimp, season with salt and pepper, and fry on both sides until golden, about 3 to 4 minutes per side.

3. Remove the shrimp from the pan and set aside on a plate. Then add the remaining 2 tablespoons butter to the pan along with the peas and minced garlic. Season as desired with salt and pepper. Cover and cook for 5 minutes, stirring occasionally, then set aside.

4. To make the sauce, melt the stick of butter in a large saucepan over medium heat. Whisk in the corn starch and cook, whisking constantly, for 2 to 4 minutes. Gradually whisk in the 4½ cups shrimp broth (saved after cooking the shrimp), making sure not to allow lumps to form. Once all the broth has been added, reduce the heat to medium-low and simmer, whisking constantly, until the sauce has thickened. Add salt and pepper to taste.

5. Spread a layer of sauce onto each plate. Add a layer of shrimp and generously sprinkle peas on top then serve.

SERVES: 2 | **PREP TIME:** 10 minutes | **COOK TIME:** 20 minutes

4 medium Yukon Gold potatoes, peeled and cut into bite-size chunks

2 medium carrots, peeled and cut into bite-size chunks

1 cup broccoli florets

3 tablespoons unsalted butter

½ cup chicken stock

½ cup cubed ham

½ cup canned crab meat or roughly chopped imitation crab

salt and pepper, to taste

⅓ cup dried bread crumbs

1½ cups shredded cheddar cheese

SEAFOOD AND VEGGIE CASSEROLE

When you think of a casserole, your first thought probably isn't "luxury." But with this Seafood and Veggie Casserole, you'd be wrong. The crab meat elevates a traditional medley of potatoes, ham, and veggies to create a casserole so rich that you'll want to a second helping before you've even finished the first.

1. Preheat the oven to 375° F.

2. Cook the potatoes and carrots in a pot of salted boiling water over medium-high heat for 10 minutes, or just before they are fork tender. Add the broccoli florets and cook for another 3 minutes.

3. Remove the vegetables from the heat and drain, then place back in the pot. Add the melted butter and chicken stock and stir to combine with the vegetables. Add the ham and crab meat, then season with salt and pepper to taste. Mix again, then distribute into 4 small gratin dishes.

4. In a small bowl, combine the bread crumbs and shredded cheese, then generously top each gratin dish with the mixture. Transfer the dishes to the oven and bake for 10 minutes before serving.

SERVES: 4 | **PREP TIME:** 5 minutes | **COOK TIME:** 25 minutes

MINI MEAT PIE

If you have some extra time on your hands, this may be the perfect time to try a Mini Meat Pie. Surrounded by flaky, buttery crust, the meat and veggies in this pie release a mouthwatering aroma as soon as you cut into it.

1. Preheat the oven to 220°F and set aside frozen puff pastry, so it has time to thaw. To make the beef cheek filling, start by mixing ½ teaspoon salt and 1 teaspoon thyme in a small bowl.

2. Remove any fat and sinew on the top layer of the beef cheeks and place them in a bowl. Rub with 1 tablespoon oil and the mixture of thyme and salt, then sprinkle each side with pepper. Place in a large nonstick frying pan over medium-high heat and fry until the meat is a dark golden-brown color, about 4 minutes per side. Set aside.

3. In a large, oven-safe saucepan over medium heat, lightly fry the celery, onion, carrot, and leek chunks. in 1 tablespoon oil until they begin to brown, about 5 minutes. Add the red wine and the beef cheeks. Boil until the alcohol evaporates, about 10 minutes, then top up with enough water to cover the cheeks.

4. Transfer the saucepan to the oven and cook for 1½ hours. Then increase the oven temperature to 280°F and cook for another 2 hours.

5. Remove from the oven and set aside to cool for 1 hour. Then remove the cheeks from the saucepan, wrap in plastic wrap, and store in the refrigerator. Discard the liquid and the vegetables in the pan.

6. While the beef cheeks are cooling, roll 1 sheet of puff pastry into a ⅛-inch-thick sheet. Transfer to the refrigerator to rest uncovered for at least 45 minutes. Once chilled, remove the pastry from the fridge and cut out 8 circles, each 5 inches across.

TIP: Leeks are grown in sandy soil and typically need extra washing to remove all of the sand and dirt. Once rinsed and cut, place the leeks in a bowl of cold water. Stir them gently with your hands for a few seconds. Any remaining sand or dirt should sink to the bottom of the bowl while the leeks float.

7. To make the shallot filling, add 1 tablespoon of oil to a frying pan over high heat. Halve the shallots lengthways, place in a small bowl, and sprinkle with salt and pepper. Then place the seasoned shallots on top of the oil with the cut side down. Caramelize the shallots until golden brown, about 7 minutes, then lower the heat to medium-low. Add the butter and thyme, cover, and cook until soft, about 4 minutes. Transfer the shallots to a small bowl, cover, and refrigerate.

8. To make the carrot and spinach filling, first halve the baby carrots lengthways. Bring a medium pot of water to boil, salt generously, and blanch the carrots for 3 to 4 minutes, or until fork tender. While they are blanching, add ice and water to a small bowl. Remove the carrots from the boiling water using a slotted spoon, dunk into the ice water for 20 to 30 seconds, and set aside.

9. Add the 3 tablespoons butter to a frying pan over medium heat. Let melt completely, then add the baby spinach and cook until slightly wilted, about 1 minute. Sprinkle with salt to taste, then transfer to a plate lined with paper towels.

10. When you are ready to construct the meat pies, remove the beef cheeks from the fridge and use your hands or a knife to break them into small chunks. Place the meat in a bowl.

11. Lay out 4 of the puff pastry circles on a flat surface. Brush with the beaten egg yolks. Add a layer of beef cheek, then blanched carrots, then wilted spinach, and lastly caramelized shallots to each pastry base.

12. Place the remaining 4 circles of pastry on top, carefully smoothing them down over the filling. Go slowly, so as not to tear the pastry. Press the edges of the top circle of pastry into the edges of the base pastry to seal each pie. Brush the tops with more of the beaten egg yolk, then chill in the fridge for 15 minutes.

13. Once chilled, remove from the fridge. To score each pie, place the edge of a knife at the top center. Make slightly curved lines down the sides, without cutting through the pastry. Seal the bottom by rolling up the pastry edges. Then use the knife to score small lines all the way around this rolled base, starting from the top and ending at the sealed edges. Return the pies to the fridge to rest for another 20 minutes.

14. While the pies are chilling, preheat the oven to 350°F. Remove the pies from the fridge and bake immediately for 20 minutes, or until the crusts are golden brown. Serve warm.

◆ ◆ ◆

SERVES: 4 | **PREP TIME:** 40 minutes + 1 hour 20 minutes for chilling | **COOK TIME:** 4 hours

FOR THE MARINATED CHICKEN:

3 tablespoons plain yogurt

1 teaspoon minced fresh ginger

1 teaspoon minced garlic

½ teaspoon salt

½ teaspoon ground turmeric

½ teaspoon red chili powder, or to taste

1 tablespoon garam masala

2 tablespoons lemon juice

1½ pounds boneless, skinless chicken breasts, cut into 1-inch cubes

CHICKEN BIRYANI

You'd be hard-pressed to find a dish more jam-packed with flavor than this delicious Chicken Biryani. Its alluring aroma alone is known to be enough to bolster one's strength and give all the energy needed to defend against roaming monsters and armored enemies alike! Just be aware that you have to plan ahead—you need to start preparing this dish the day before you get to enjoy it.

1. Start by marinating the chicken the day before you plan to cook it. In a large mixing bowl, add all the ingredients for the marinade (not including the chicken) and mix well. Then place the chicken in the marinade and mix until every cube is thoroughly coated. Cover the bowl with plastic wrap or a large plate and refrigerate overnight.

FOR ASSEMBLING THE BIRYANI:

1 tablespoon ghee

1 onion, chopped

1 jalapeño pepper, diced

2 tablespoons minced fresh ginger

2 teaspoons garam masala

1 teaspoon ground turmeric

1 teaspoon ground cumin

1 teaspoon salt

3 cloves garlic, minced

2 large Roma tomatoes, chopped

½ cup golden raisins

2 cups chicken broth

¼ cup water

1 cup uncooked basmati rice

fresh cilantro, chopped, for serving

1 green onion, chopped, for serving

1 lime, cut into wedges, for serving

2. To make the biryani, start by adding 1 tablespoon ghee to a large saucepan or Dutch oven over medium-high heat. When melted, add the marinated chicken pieces and cook until golden brown, about 5 minutes.

3. Flip the chicken pieces and add the jalapeño, onion, ginger, garam masala, turmeric, cumin, and salt. Sauté until the onions start turning translucent, about 3 minutes.

4. Add the garlic, tomatoes, and raisins, then stir to combine. Pour in the chicken broth, water, and rice. Bring to a boil, then reduce heat to medium-low. Cover with a lid and let cook for 15 minutes.

5. Turn off the heat and use a fork to mix the rice. Cover again and let sit for another 10 minutes without heat so the rice can fully cook.

6. Transfer biryani to a serving dish and top with cilantro and green onions. Squeeze some lime juice over the top, then garnish the plate with remaining lime wedges and serve.

✦ ✦ ✦

SERVES: 4 | **PREP TIME:** 10 minutes + overnight marinating | **COOK TIME:** 35 minutes

Ingredients

2 pounds shrimp, peeled and deveined, tails on

1 teaspoon salt

1 teaspoon black pepper

1 teaspoon garlic powder

5 tablespoons curry powder, divided

2 tablespoons olive oil

1 onion, halved and then sliced

2 red bell peppers, sliced

3 cloves garlic, minced

1 teaspoon minced fresh ginger

1 teaspoon ground turmeric

1 teaspoon ground cumin

¼ teaspoon cayenne pepper, or to taste

1½ cups chicken stock

1 teaspoon dried thyme

1 (13.5-ounce) can coconut milk

3 russet potatoes, peeled and chopped into bite-size pieces

cooked long grain rice, for serving

fresh parsley, chopped for serving

CREAMY SHRIMP CURRY

Next time you're at the local market, find a stall selling fresh seafood and pick up a few pounds of shrimp to make this Creamy Shrimp Curry. You won't regret it! People say that some plates of food convey feelings of passion and warmth, and this is one of those dishes. Harmonious spices blend with creamy coconut milk to create a bright flavor that none of your travel companions can say no to!

1. In a medium bowl, season the shrimp with the salt, pepper, garlic powder, and 2 tablespoons curry powder. Mix until all the shrimp are thoroughly coated. Cover and place in the refrigerator.

2. In a large pot over medium-high heat, heat the olive oil for about 2 minutes. Add the sliced onions and peppers and sauté for 5 minutes, or until the peppers have softened and the onions are turning translucent.

3. Stir in the garlic and ginger and cook until fragrant, about 1 minute. Season with remaining curry powder, turmeric, cumin, and cayenne pepper. Reduce the heat to medium-low and continue sautéing for 2 to 3 minutes.

4. Add the chicken stock and thyme and stir to combine. While mixing, pour in the coconut milk. Turn the heat back up to medium-high and bring the mixture to a boil. Add the potatoes, cover with a lid, and cook until the potatoes are fork tender, about 7 minutes.

5. Remove the shrimp from the refrigerator and add to the pot, stirring to combine. Cover and cook for 5 minutes, or until the shrimp are fully pink.

6. Remove the pot from the heat. Serve the shrimp curry over rice, sprinkled with chopped parsley.

SERVES: 4 | **PREP TIME:** 10 minutes | **COOK TIME:** 30 minutes

1 (6-ounce) package rice tagliatelle noodles

3 tablespoons olive oil

½ onion, sliced

1 green bell pepper, sliced

1 red bell pepper, sliced

3 cloves garlic, minced

1 teaspoon hoisin sauce

2 tablespoons soy sauce

1 (8-ounce) tilapia fillet, cut into 1-inch pieces

salt and pepper, to taste

FISH AND NOODLE STIR FRY

When you're feeling a little tired of the typical meats and veggies cooked over the campfire, it's time to give this delicious dinner a try. The springy rice noodles add a balance of texture when paired with pieces of soft, flaky tilapia. Stir-fried with the best fresh ingredients and savory oils and sauces you can find, this dish is one you'll want to keep coming back to!

1. Cook the rice noodles according to the package instructions. Drain and set aside.

2. Add the oil to a wok or large frying pan over medium-high heat. Heat for about 2 minutes and then add the onion and bell peppers slices. Sauté for 3 minutes, stirring frequently.

3. Stir in the garlic, hoisin sauce, and soy sauce and cook for 1 minute.

4. Season the tilapia pieces with salt and pepper and add to the pan. Cook for 2 to 3 minutes, stirring frequently so the fish doesn't burn.

5. Add the rice noodles and toss gently so the noodles are thoroughly coated and mixed with the veggies. Serve immediately!

SERVES: 2 | **PREP TIME:** 10 minutes | **COOK TIME:** 15 minutes

½ cup plain yogurt

1½ teaspoons lemon juice

3 cloves garlic, minced

1 tablespoon minced
fresh ginger

2 teaspoons garam masala

1 teaspoon ground turmeric

1 teaspoon ground cumin

1 teaspoon red chili powder

1 teaspoon salt

1½ pounds boneless,
skinless chicken breasts,
cut into bite-size cubes

CREAMY BUTTER CHICKEN

The marinade in this recipe makes for a plate of the juiciest chicken you can imagine. With its symphony of spices and thick, creamy sauce, Creamy Butter Chicken might just be one of the favorite recipes you've gathered on your journey. There's no chance your plate won't be clean by the end of the meal!

1. In a large mixing bowl combine the marinade ingredients (not including the chicken), and mix well. Add the cubed chicken and mix again. Let the chicken marinate in the mixture for at least 30 minutes, or overnight. (If marinating overnight, cover the bowl and refrigerate.)

2. To make the Butter Chicken, in a large pot or Dutch oven, heat the ghee over medium-high heat. When it sizzles, add chicken pieces so the bottom of the pan is covered but not crowded. Fry until browned, about 3 minutes on each side, then transfer to a shallow dish and cover to keep warm. Repeat until all the chicken pieces have been cooked.

3. Add the olive oil to the same pot and sauté the chopped onions in the oil over medium-high heat until translucent, about 4 minutes.

4. Add the garlic and ginger and sauté for 1 more minute, until fragrant. Sprinkle in the ground coriander, cumin, and garam masala and cook, stirring constantly until fragrant, about 30 seconds.

5. Add the crushed tomatoes, chili powder, and salt. Stir everything together and lightly scrape the pan to incorporate any spices stuck to the bottom. Let simmer for 15 minutes, stirring occasionally.

FOR THE BUTTER CHICKEN:

2 tablespoons ghee

1 tablespoon olive oil

1 onion, finely chopped

3 cloves garlic, minced

1 tablespoon minced fresh ginger

1 teaspoon ground coriander

2 teaspoons ground cumin

2 teaspoons garam masala

1 (15-ounce) can crushed tomatoes

½ teaspoon red chili powder

1¼ teaspoons salt

1 cup heavy cream

1 tablespoon sugar

½ teaspoon crushed kasoori methi (dried fenugreek leaves)

FOR SERVING:

2 cups jasmine rice, rinsed

4 cups water

salt, to taste

fresh parsley or cilantro, chopped, for serving

SPECIAL EQUIPMENT

immersion blender

6. Turn off the heat and use an immersion blender to blend the sauce in the pot. Stir in the cream, sugar, and kasoori methi. Add the chicken and all its juices back into the sauce and cook over medium heat for 8 to 10 minutes, until the chicken is cooked through and the sauce has thickened.

7. While the sauce is thickening, cook the rice. Add two cups of rinsed jasmine rice and 4 cups water to a medium pot over medium heat. Bring to a boil, then lightly salt the water, reduce heat to low, stir, and cover with a lid. Cook until all the water has absorbed, and the rice is fluffy, about 15 minutes.

8. Transfer rice to a serving dish and top with the butter chicken. Garnish with chopped parsley or cilantro and serve.

◆ ◆ ◆

SERVES: 4 | **PREP TIME:** 15 minutes + 30 minutes or more for marinating | **COOK TIME:** 30 minutes

DRINKS & DESSERTS

Ingredients

2 teaspoons gelatin powder

2 cups water, divided

1 cup fresh spearmint leaves + more, for serving

green food coloring

2 tablespoon lemon juice

2 cups sugar

REFRESHING JELLIED MINT

This deliciously light dish is the perfect after-dinner dessert. Its clean and crisp mint flavor will cleanse your palate and leave you energized for whatever comes next. You'll know you've made a perfect Refreshing Jellied Mint if the jelly springs back with a happy jiggle when tapped gently with a spoon.

1. Place the gelatin powder in a small bowl and add enough of the water to cover it, about ¼ cup. Let it soak—but don't stir!

2. Place the 1 cup spearmint leaves in a stock pot along with the remaining water. Bring to a boil over high heat, then remove from the heat, cover, and let sit for 10 minutes.

3. Pour spearmint tea through a fine-mesh strainer. Add more water if necessary to equal 2 cups. Return the liquid to the stock pot.

4. Add green food coloring until you achieve your desired color. Add lemon juice and sugar and stir until the sugar is dissolved. If necessary, simmer for 3 to 4 minutes to help the sugar dissolve.

5. Remove the pot from the heat and allow the mixture to cool to 140°F, about 30 to 40 minutes. Then add the soaked gelatin and stir until dissolved.

6. Pour the mixture into 2 rounded bowls and refrigerate until set, about 5 hours.

7. To remove the jelly from the bowls, soak them in hot water. To do this, pour 1 or 2 inches of hot water into a larger bowl. Then set a jelly bowl gently into the hot water, being careful not to get water into the jelly bowl! Let sit for 2 to 3 minutes, then remove the jelly bowl, place a serving plate over it, turn upside down, and shake slightly to help the jelly fall onto the plate. Repeat for the second bowl.

8. Garnish with fresh spearmint leaves and serve.

◆ ◆ ◆

SERVES: 2 | **PREP TIME:** 20 minutes | **COOK TIME:** 10 minutes + 5 hours cooling/setting time

THE UNOFFICIAL GENSHIN IMPACT COOKBOOK

2 tablespoons potato starch

1 tablespoon sugar

¾ cup water

1 banana, sliced

FRUIT MANJU

When the heat of summer or the intensity of the battlefield is getting to be too much, this is the ideal dish to help you cool off and recharge. Fresh fruit encased in a sweet gelatin makes for the perfect bite every time. While bananas are called for in this recipe, for this delectable dessert you can use any fresh fruit you've collected during your travels!

1. In a saucepan over medium-low heat, combine the potato starch, sugar, and ¾ cup water. Using a wire whisk, stir frequently until the liquid becomes a translucent jelly, about 5 minutes.

2. Spoon the warm jelly into a silicone or nonstick mini muffin tin until the cups are about ⅔ full. Add the sliced banana, then spoon more warm jelly on top. Make sure that no parts of the banana are poking up through the jelly.

3. Refrigerate for 1 hour, then gently pop the manju onto a plate to serve.

◆ ◆ ◆

SERVES: 2 | **PREP TIME:** 5 minutes | **COOK TIME:** 5 minutes + 1 hour refrigerating time

6 pickled sakura leaves

1 tablespoon glutinous rice flour

¼ cup + 2 teaspoons water

6 tablespoons all-purpose flour

1 tablespoon sugar

red food coloring

4 ounces red bean paste

oil, for greasing pan

sakura blossoms, for serving (optional)

TIP: Pickled sakura leaves can easily be found and bought online or at your local Asian market. They have a unique floral flavor with both sweet and salty hints, a taste you can't find anywhere else.

SPRINGTIME MOCHI

Nothing says springtime quite like cherry blossom petals blowing in a light breeze. But if your travels have taken you to a place devoid of sakura trees, never fear! Celebrate cherry blossom season and the coming of spring with a delicious mochi recipe. The color of this Springtime Mochi will remind you of sweet cherry blossoms and make you feel as if you've just spent a fine spring morning perched under a sakura tree.

1. Soak the sakura leaves in a bowl of water for 10 minutes. Pat dry with paper towels and set aside.

2. In a medium bowl, combine the rice flour and ¼ cup + 2 teaspoons water and whisk until well blended. Sift in the all-purpose flour, add sugar, and whisk again until well combined.

3. Add the red food coloring, just enough to make the mixture pink. Begin with 1 drop, mix well, and add another drop if the cooler seems too light.

4. Divide the bean paste into 6 even portions and roll them into ½-inch thick logs.

5. Lightly grease a nonstick frying pan with oil and heat over medium-low heat.

6. Using a spoon, gently pour some of the mochi batter into the pan, spreading the mixture with the spoon to form an oval about 5 inches long and 2 inches wide. Cook for 10 to 15 seconds, until the top surface is dry. Immediately flip and cook for 5 to 10 seconds more. Repeat until you have 6 mochi ovals.

7. Roll each mochi oval around a log of red bean paste. Then roll each in a pickled sakura leaf and top each mochi roll with a sakura blossom if you have them. Arrange on a plate to serve.

SERVES: 6 | **PREP TIME:** 15 minutes | **COOK TIME:** 5 minutes

½ cup rice flour

½ cup powdered sugar

1 cup glutinous
(sweet) rice flour

1 cup cold soy milk

1 to 2 tablespoons milk
or water, if needed

2 drops red food coloring

½ teaspoon matcha
(green tea) powder

SPECIAL EQUIPMENT
5 bamboo skewers

COLORFUL DANGO

If you ever find yourself walking around a breezy summer festival, chances are someone will be selling this Colorful Dango, and you'll want to grab a stick (or two)! The sweet taste and vibrant colors are the perfect combination, reminding you to savor the easy summer days before the next big adventure begins.

1. Soak the bamboo skewers in cold water for at least 30 minutes.

2. In a large bowl, combine the rice flour, powdered sugar, glutinous rice flour, and soy milk. On a flat surface, knead into a smooth dough. Add 1 to 2 tablespoons of milk or water if the dough feels too dry or falls apart.

3. Divide the dough into 3 equal portions. Add 2 drops red food coloring to 1 portion of dough, add the matcha powder to another portion, and leave the third portion white.

4. Knead each piece of dough, making sure the food coloring and matcha powder are evenly distributed. Then divide each portion into 5 equal pieces and roll them into round balls.

5. Bring a medium pot of water to a boil over high heat. Boil the dango balls over medium heat for about 15 minutes, or until they are floating. (You can do this in one batch—the white dango balls won't be colored by the other balls.)

6. Fill a large bowl with ice water and use a slotted spoon to transfer the cooked dango balls to the bowl. Let them cool in the water until you're ready to put them onto the skewers.

7. Insert 3 cooled dango balls onto each bamboo skewer in the order of green, white, and pink. Hand them out and enjoy!

◆ ◆ ◆

SERVES: 5 | **PREP TIME:** 35 minutes | **COOK TIME:** 15 minutes

1 cup shelled almonds

4 cups water

2 teaspoons agar-agar powder

¼ cup granulated sugar

1 tablespoon osmanthus syrup (or elderberry flower syrup)

SPECIAL EQUIPMENT
nut milk bag or cheesecloth

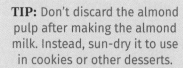

TIP: Don't discard the almond pulp after making the almond milk. Instead, sun-dry it to use in cookies or other desserts.

SWEET ALMOND TOFU

Passing through a local inn, you just might come across a rather reserved man known as a defender against demons, enjoying his favorite dish in solitude. This dessert, named for its tofu-like appearance and silky texture despite containing no tofu, is capable of lifting anyone's spirits. Enjoy it with friends or by yourself—the first bite will drive away any personal demons and leave you feeling ready to take on the world!

1. Add the almonds to a bowl of water and let soak in the refrigerator for at least 6 hours, or overnight.

2. Drain the soaked almonds and place in a blender with 4 cups of water. Blend until smooth, then use a nut milk bag or a cheesecloth to strain the almond milk into a medium cooking pot. Set the almond pulp aside.

3. In a medium pot over medium-high heat, combine the agar-agar powder and sugar with the almond milk. Bring to a boil, then lower the heat and simmer until the agar-agar is completely dissolved, about 5 minutes.

4. Pour the mixture into a square dish so you can cut it in cubes later. Set aside to cool to room temperature, then transfer to the fridge until completely cooled, about 2 hours.

5. Remove the dish from the fridge, transfer the almond tofu to a plate, and cut into large cubes. Drizzle with osmanthus syrup to serve.

◆ ◆ ◆

SERVES: 2 | **PREP TIME:** 10 minutes + 6 hours soaking and 2 hours chilling time | **COOK TIME:** 10 minutes

- 1½ cups water
- ¾ cup uncooked white rice
- 2 cups whole milk, divided
- ⅓ cup sugar
- ¼ teaspoon salt
- 1 egg, beaten
- 1 tablespoon unsalted butter
- ½ teaspoon pure vanilla extract
- ground cinnamon, for serving
- sliced mango, for serving
- fresh mint, for serving

STICKY RICE PUDDING

It can take months of hard adventuring (and dedicated farming for character level-up materials) to build up the stamina to climb that tall mountain or dodge enemy attacks in a long battle. That's where this recipe comes in. Sticky Rice Pudding, with its creamy texture and sweet flavor, will give you that extra boost of stamina you may need as you work on becoming the best adventurer you can be.

1. In a medium saucepan over medium heat, bring the water to a boil. Once boiling, stir in the rice and immediately reduce the heat to low. Cover and let simmer until the liquid is absorbed, about 20 minutes.

2. Add 1½ cups milk to the saucepan along with the sugar and salt. Turn the heat back up to medium and stir until well combined. Continue stirring occasionally and cook until the rice mixture becomes thick and creamy, about 15 minutes.

3. Add the remaining ½ cup milk and the beaten egg and cook for 2 minutes, stirring constantly. Remove from the heat and stir in the butter and vanilla until well combined.

4. Divide the rice pudding into 4 bowls. Sprinkle with cinnamon and top with mango slices and fresh mint. Serve warm.

◆ ◆ ◆

SERVE: 4 | **PREP TIME:** 10 minutes | **COOK TIME:** 40 minutes

FRAGRANT ROSE CUSTARD

3 cups whole milk, divided

6 tablespoons sugar

3 tablespoons vanilla custard powder

2 teaspoons rose water

¼ cup pureed fresh strawberries

peeled pistachios, chopped, for serving

edible flowers, such as roses and violets, for serving

This floral dessert will cleanse your palate and leave you feeling refreshed after any meal. The subtle hints of rose elevate your typical creamy custard to a dish fit to grace the tables of even the wealthiest diners. The dusting of pistachios and sprinkling of flowers also helps with that!

1. In a heavy-bottom pan over medium-high heat, bring 2 cups of milk to a boil. Add the sugar, reduce the heat to medium-low, and stir until the sugar is dissolved.

2. Mix the custard powder into the remaining 1 cup milk, whisking until there are no lumps. Pour the mixture into the boiled milk and continue mixing over medium heat for 5 to 6 minutes, or until the mixture thickens.

3. Remove from the heat and, using a rubber spatula, gently fold in the strawberry puree and rose water until well combined. Pour into 2 medium bowls and refrigerate for at least 1 hour before serving.

4. Top with chopped pistachios and edible flowers to serve.

◆ ◆ ◆

SERVES: 2 | **PREP TIME:** 5 minutes | **COOK TIME:** 10 minutes + 1 hour chilling time

FOR THE DOUGH:

1½ cups all-purpose flour, divided

4⅓ tablespoons unsalted butter, divided

1 tablespoon sugar

11 teaspoons water + red food coloring

vegetable oil, for frying

FOR THE MARZIPAN:

¾ cup almond flour

10 tablespoons powdered sugar

4 teaspoons water

½ teaspoon almond extract

CRISPY LOTUS FLOWERS

Despite the name of this dish, you won't find any real flowers here. Instead, you'll be putting all the culinary skills you've acquired on your travels to the test by using simple ingredients to create a sweet dessert that celebrates the beauty of the lotus flower. Is there truly anything better than a deep-fried dessert?

1. To make the white dough, in a medium bowl, mix ¾ cup of the flour with 2⅔ tablespoons of the butter. Knead until smooth and cover with plastic wrap. Set aside for 30 minutes.

2. To make the red dough, mix another ¾ cup flour with 1⅔ tablespoons butter. Work in 1 tablespoon sugar and the red water mixture. Mix well and knead until a smooth dough is formed. Cover with plastic wrap and set aside for 30 minutes.

3. Add all the marzipan ingredients to a medium bowl and mix until well combined.

4. Divide the white dough, the red dough, and the marzipan each into 9 equal-size balls.

5. Using a rolling pin, flatten the red balls into circles. Wrap a white dough ball with a red dough circle, covering it entirely. Repeat with each red dough circle and white dough ball.

6. Squash down each red/white dough ball and use a rolling pin to flatten it into an oval. Roll up into a ball once again and cover with plastic wrap for 15 minutes.

7. Repeat Step 6, flattening the rolled dough into ovals, rolling them back into balls, then letting them rest for 15 minutes, covered with plastic wrap.

8. After the dough has rested, remove the plastic wrap and use your thumb to press each piece of dough into a bowl shape, letting the edges tilt up and onward the middle. Place a marzipan ball in the middle of each dough bowl, then wrap the dough edges around it to seal in the marzipan and form a ball.

9. Place the sealed side of the ball face down, then cut a star shape in the top surface of the ball, cutting only deep enough so you can just see the marzipan filling.

10. Fill a deep saucepan or fryer halfway with vegetable oil and heat to 300°F. Place a lotus ball in a mesh strainer and lower it into the oil to fry. Cook 1 or 2 lotus balls at a time. Use a ladle to pour hot oil onto the balls, letting it bloom and create some layers. Each ball needs to cook around 3 to 4 minutes in the hot oil.

11. Place the cooked lotus flower crisps on a paper towel-lined plate to drain the oil. Allow to cool fully and then enjoy!

◆ ◆ ◆

SERVES: 2 | **PREP TIME:** 15 minutes | **COOK TIME:** 10 minutes

FOR THE BAKLAVA:

1 cup (2 sticks) unsalted butter, melted

1 (16-ounce) package frozen phyllo dough, thawed

1½ cup shelled pistachios

1½ cup shelled walnuts

1½ cup shelled almonds

¼ cup sugar

1 tablespoon ground cinnamon

⅓ teaspoon ground cloves

ground pistachios, for serving

FOR THE HONEY SYRUP:

1 cup sugar

1 cup cold water

½ cup honey

5 whole cloves

juice if 1 lemon

RESTORING BAKLAVA

Households everywhere—from lush green forests to arid deserts—love to serve this aromatic dessert. It's said that even great scholars are in need of this baklava before exams to give them that extra boost of energy. Nutty, buttery goodness meets the sharp sweetness of honey to create a truly unforgettable dessert.

1. Preheat the oven to 350°F. Brush a 9 x 13-inch baking pan with a small amount of the melted butter for the baklava and set aside. Unroll the thawed pastry dough, place between kitchen towels, and set aside on a flat surface.

2. To make the honey syrup, add the 1 cup sugar and 1 cup water to a small saucepan over medium-high heat. Stir until the sugar dissolves, then add the honey and cloves and stir again. Bring to a boil, then reduce to low heat and simmer for 20 minutes. Remove from the heat and let cool. When the syrup reaches room temperature, remove the cloves and add the lemon juice. Stir to combine and set aside.

3. To make the baklava, start by creating a nut mixture. Using a food processor, pulse the pistachios, walnuts, and almonds a couple of times until finely chopped. Transfer the mixture to a medium bowl and stir in the ¼ cup sugar, cinnamon, and ground cloves.

4. To assemble the baklava, place a sheet of phyllo pastry in the bottom of your prepared baking dish. Trim any excess edges, then brush the dough with melted butter.

5. Repeat this process until half of the phyllo pastry sheets have been used and each new layer has been brushed with melted butter. Then sprinkle the nut mixture over the top layer of pastry. Then continue assembling with the rest of phyllo pastry sheets and melted butter.

6. In the baking dish, cut the baklava into small squares. Bake on the middle oven rack for 35 to 45 minutes, or until golden brown on top.

7. Remove the baklava from the oven and immediately pour the honey syrup over the top.

8. Let cool for at least 2 hours, or overnight, uncovered, at room temperature. Sprinkle with ground pistachios to serve.

◆ ◆ ◆

SERVES: 6 | **PREP TIME:** 30 minutes | **COOK TIME:** 35 to 45 minutes + 2 hours for cooling

1 bag black tea

½ cup hot water

1 cup ice, divided

1 tablespoon lemon juice

1 tablespoon maple syrup, or to taste

½ cup mixed berries, for serving

sliced lemon, for serving

SPECIAL EQUIPMENT
cocktail shaker

EVENING FRUIT TEA

This delightful tea has a dual personality. While sipping this drink may make you feel as if you're sitting on a grassy hill catching the last rays of a summer sunset, it also packs a punch that can get you up and ready to tackle your next gliding lesson, or help you stay up late studying the adventurer's handbook. Garnish your tea with a flare of red (like a red flower or red tiki umbrella) to pay homage to everyone's favorite outrider.

1. Heat water on the stovetop over medium-high heat and remove it just before it starts to boil, or use an electric kettle with a temperature setting. If using electric kettle, set the water temperature to 190°F.

2. Place the tea bag in a teapot or mug and pour in ½ cup of the hot water. Cover and steep for 3 minutes, then discard the tea bag.

3. Add the hot tea, ½ cup of ice, lemon juice, and maple syrup to a cocktail shaker. Shake for 20 seconds.

4. Pour the mixture into a glass filled with the remaining ice. Add the berries on top and garnish with sliced lemon.

✦ ✦ ✦

SERVES: 1 | **PREP TIME:** 1 minute | **COOK TIME:** 3 minutes

FESTIVAL FRUIT MOCKTAIL

2 tablespoons
unsweetened banana juice

1 tablespoon freshly
squeezed lemon juice

1 tablespoon jasmine syrup

ice

2 tablespoons lychee juice

1 tablespoon blue
curaçao syrup

SPECIAL EQUIPMENT
cocktail shaker

Who says you need alcohol to enjoy a festival? Travelers need to keep their wits about them, even when celebrating at a festival with close friends. Shaken up with unique fruit flavors and a hint of floral syrup, this mocktail is bursting with summer flavors and bright colors that are sure to keep the spirit of summer alive.

1. Add the banana and lemon juices, jasmine syrup, and a handful of ice to a cocktail shaker. Shake for 20 seconds, then strain into a tulip glass (if available) filled with ice.

2. Add the lychee juice, blue curaçao syrup, and another handful of ice to the cocktail shaker. Shake for 10 seconds, then gently pour over the banana juice mixture so that it floats on top.

3. Decorate with whatever festival-related garnishes you may have on hand!

SERVES: 1 | **PREP TIME:** 5 minutes

Ingredients

5 medium apples of your choice, peeled and roughly chopped

½ orange, peeled and quartered

2 cinnamon sticks

½ teaspoon whole cloves

2 teaspoons minced fresh ginger

8 cups water

¼ cup maple syrup

apple slices, for serving

fresh mint leaves, for serving

FRESH APPLE CIDER

A refreshing drink that can be served hot or cold, Fresh Apple Cider is famous for its seemingly magical ability to sober anyone up with just a few sips. Maybe that's why this drink is so popular with the patrons of a certain winery.

1. In a large stockpot, add the apples, oranges, cinnamon, cloves, and ginger. Pour in 8 cups water.

2. Bring to a boil over high heat. Then reduce the heat to medium-low, cover with a lid, and simmer for 1 hour, or until the apples are fork tender.

3. Using a potato masher, lightly crush the apples and oranges to extract more flavor. Cover the pot again and simmer for 1 more hour.

4. Using a fine-mesh strainer, scoop out and discard the apples, oranges, and spices. Stir in the maple syrup.

5. Serve the cider warm, or allow it to cool and serve in glasses filled with ice. Garnish with fresh apple slices and mint leaves.

◆ ◆ ◆

SERVES: 6 | **PREP TIME:** 10 minutes | **COOK TIME:** 3 hours

CONVERSIONS

VOLUME

U.S.	U.S. Equivalent	Metric
1 tablespoon (3 teaspoons)	½ fluid ounce	15 milliliters
¼ cup	2 fluid ounces	60 milliliters
⅓ cup	3 fluid ounces	90 milliliters
½ cup	4 fluid ounces	120 milliliters
⅔ cup	5 fluid ounces	150 milliliters
¾ cup	6 fluid ounces	180 milliliters
1 cup	8 fluid ounces	240 milliliters
2 cups	16 fluid ounces	480 milliliters

WEIGHT

U.S.	Metric
½ ounce	15 grams
1 ounce	30 grams
2 ounces	60 grams
¼ pound	115 grams
⅓ pound	150 grams
½ pound	225 grams
¾ pound	350 grams
1 pound	450 grams

TEMPERATURE

Fahrenheit (°F)	Celsius (°C)	Fahrenheit (°F)	Celsius (°C)
70°F	20°C	220°F	105°C
100°F	40°C	240°F	115°C
120°F	50°C	260°F	125°C
130°F	55°C	280°F	140°C
140°F	60°C	300°F	150°C
150°F	65°C	325°F	165°C
160°F	70°C	350°F	175°C
170°F	75°C	375°F	190°C
180°F	80°C	400°F	200°C
190°F	90°C	425°F	220°C
200°F	95°C	450°F	230°C

ABOUT THE CONTRIBUTORS

Kierra Sondereker is an associate editor for Ulysses Press and lives in Brooklyn, New York. On a typical day, you can find her playing Genshin Impact (she's currently AR 59) or Animal Crossing, discovering a new K-drama, or finding the best happy hours in her neighborhood. Kierra is the author of *Mixology and Murder*, a true crime cocktail book.

Nevyana Dimitrova is a professional food photographer who has had a love of cooking since she was a little girl. She tells stories through the food she prepares and captures in photos. The magic of nature inspires her constantly, and she always works with absolute passion on her creations.